10 Lifesavers for Every Couple

Dr. David Hawkins
THE RELATIONSHIP DOCTOR

HARVEST HOUSE PUBLISHERS
EUGENE, OREGON

All Scripture quotations are taken from the HOLY BIBLE, NEW INTERNATIONAL VERSION®. NIV®. Copyright © 1973, 1978, 1984 by the International Bible Society. Used by permission of Zondervan. All rights reserved.

Cover by Koechel Peterson & Associates, Inc., Minneapolis, Minnesota

Cover photo © Fancy/Veer/Corbis

This book contains stories in which people's identities and some details of their situations have been changed to protect their privacy.

10 LIFESAVERS FOR EVERY COUPLE

Published by Harvest House Publishers
Eugene, Oregon 97402
www.harvesthousepublishers.com

Library of Congress Cataloging-in-Publication Data
Hawkins, David, 1951-
10 lifesavers for every couple / David Hawkins.
p. cm.
ISBN 978-0-7369-2284-5 (pbk.)
1. Spouses—Religious life. 2. Marital conflict—Religious aspects—Christianity. I. Title. II. Title: 10 lifesavers for every couple.
BV4596.M3H394 2009
248.8'44—dc22

2008020673

Printed in the United States of America

09 10 11 12 13 14 15 16 17 / BP-SK / 10 9 8 7 6 5 4 3 2 1

Contents

1

Recognizing a State of Emergency

Your seat cushions can be used for floatation,
and in the event of an emergency water landing,
please take them with our compliments.

AIRLINE ADVISORY

Sirens scream and lights flash as the ambulance streaks down the road, vehicles scrambling to get out of the way. I grip the steering wheel with both hands and maneuver to the side of the road, allowing the emergency medical van to pass.

I'm on red alert—my senses tuned in, my eyes scanning the area for whatever might happen next. Blood rushes to my brain, and I'm ready for action. My fight-or-flight response is fully functional.

The ambulance passes, and I breathe a sigh of relief. I fear for those experiencing a medical crisis, but I know that the trained medics in the back of the ambulance will take immediate measures. The hospital has been alerted, and doctors and nurses are standing by, ready to begin emergency treatment.

As the siren fades into the distance, I pull back onto the road. This time, the siren wasn't for me. Aside from a momentary panic, I'm fine.

Or am I?

We've memorized the phone number to call when gravely ill. But what do we do when we're faced with a marital emergency? What if our relationship is in critical danger? Do we even recognize when we're in a marital emergency or know where to turn for help? Does the marriage simply collapse, leaving us in need of emergency marital CPR?

During more than 30 years of counseling, I have found that most people don't know what to do when their marriage is in serious distress. Most believe they will never experience a marital crisis. After all, they pledged to love their mate "until death us do part."

But marital emergencies happen, and you need to be prepared if one happens to you. This book is about the cold, hard truth that most couples go through times of intense difficulty. Some relationships don't survive. Although we intend for our marriage to last forever and desire to love our mate until the end of time, often this is not what happens.

If you're tempted to close the pages of this book because you think I'm being too harsh, I want to make one thing clear—although emergencies are likely to happen in your marriage, lifesavers are available. Rather than being the death knell to your relationship, a crisis can be a productive time for examining what you've been doing wrong. If you correct your mistakes, you can enjoy a future filled with love and possibility.

Couples in Crisis

Most couples experience some kind of marital crisis. Unfortunately, most aren't prepared—and that is the purpose of this book. *10 Lifesavers for Every Couple* is the relationship equivalent of your AAA card. It is like the bracelet you wear on your wrist if you're a diabetic. This manual just might save your relationship.

With physical ailments, we can often predict problems because of one or more of the following symptoms:

pain
heart palpitations
swelling or tissue change
weight gain or loss

sleep disturbance

physiological changes

If you were to experience any of these symptoms, you'd take notice. Although you might want to deny the severity of the situation, you'd be forced to take action if the symptoms persisted. And you'd have some idea about where to turn for help in dealing with this medical emergency.

Marital emergencies can also be predicted by various symptoms. Yet far too many couples slip into a crisis without seeing it coming. Failing to recognize the warning signs, most never turn to anyone for help.

"I didn't see it coming," one woman told me recently after her husband of 15 years asked for a separation.

"I knew we had some problems," she continued, "but certainly not enough to cause him to leave our marriage."

Sherry was kind and soft-spoken. Deep circles under her eyes indicated she was not sleeping well. Her long brown hair was pulled back with a clip, and her outfit appeared thrown together. She cried easily as she talked about her husband, their marriage, and two preteen children.

"I just didn't see it coming," she repeated. "We've been active in our church, and I thought we were both completely committed to each other."

"Why don't you to start by giving me a little history," I suggested. "And then we'll focus on how you can cope and what you might be able to do about saving your marriage."

Sherry told she'd met her husband during their college years at a youth Bible camp, where they worked as counselors. They became fast friends during their first year of counseling and started dating during their second summer at camp.

Sherry fidgeted with her hair as she looked out the window and muttered something under her breath. Sensing the urgency of the situation, I decided to help her focus on the present problem.

"What's happening between you two right now?" I asked.

She paused, continuing to look out the window onto the slow-moving river across the street. She seemed lost for a moment and then began to cry again.

"He doesn't want to talk to me," she said. "He's asking for time to think things over. He says he doesn't want to be mean, but he's not sure how he feels about me."

"Has he been more specific than that?" I asked. "Has he indicated what problems led to this stage?"

"He says he's been struggling for some time but hasn't known how to tell me. He's tired of our bickering, but I didn't think it was that bad. I know he hates conflict."

"That's still pretty vague," I said. "He's not mentioned anything else that's bothering him?"

"Not really," she said. "He's just tired of fighting about the way we raise our kids and the way we spend money. He feels like he works too hard not to be further ahead than we are, and he thinks I spend money foolishly, which might be true. I just want to figure this out and do whatever I can to save our marriage. He means everything to me, and I certainly don't want our children to be raised in a broken home."

"We'll figure out what happened," I said, "but we also need to help you prepare for the days and weeks to come. Do you have support in your life—any friends or family who will help you cope with what you're going through?"

"My best friend has been there for me," she said. "And my mom has also been great."

"That's important," I said. "Working on your marriage, even though he's left, requires you to be able to cope emotionally and physically."

"It's a shock," she said. "I need to understand why this happened."

"Understanding what happened and how this crisis started is important," I said. "But making smart decisions on how to interact with him now, if that's possible, might be even more important.

Maybe if we can determine his point of need we can figure out what needs to be done to save the marriage."

As is often the case in an emergency, Sherry is uncertain how to proceed. She never considered this could happen to her. She needs guidance and wisdom if she is to have a chance at saving her marriage.

Sherry's situation is not unusual. Couples of all ages are experiencing severe turmoil—marriage crises—and are uncertain about what to do to stabilize and strengthen their marriage. Marriages end in divorce more than 50 percent of the time, largely because couples are not prepared to deal with these marital emergencies. Because of generations of divorce, many couples wonder about even marrying in the first place. We're unraveling stitch by stitch, and we are in desperate need of emergency marriage repair.

Don and Brittany

Don and Brittany are another couple experiencing an emergency. Married for 20 years, they still have not worked out the bugs and settled into a pleasant relationship.

Walking stiffly into my office, they chose chairs as far from each other as possible. Dressed in khakis and polo shirt, Don curtly stated that he had taken part of the day off from his job as an insurance agent to attend this counseling session. He made it clear that he expected me to get down to business so he could return to work as quickly as possible.

Brittany had come straight from the hospital and was dressed in her nursing scrubs. Angry and sullen, she glared at Don when he spoke.

"Our relationship has been rocky, off and on, since the beginning," Don offered. "I don't think Brittany fights fair, and it's been going on too long. She's moody and seems angry most of the time. I'm the one who insisted that we get help, but quite honestly, I've got mixed feelings about being here. I don't know that she's willing to make any changes."

"How does it look from your angle?" I asked Brittany.

"I agree with the rocky part," she said. "We can't seem to have a conversation without it erupting into World War III. He's always complaining about the way I talk to him, but I think he talks to me just as harshly as I talk to him."

"At least you agree that it's hard to communicate and that you fight about far too many things," I offered.

Both nodded, still as stiff and uncomfortable as the moment they had arrived.

"So what finally motivated you to seek help?" I asked. "Has something in particular provided the impetus?"

"I just told her it was time," Don said. "Enough is enough. I'm tired of living this way. Either we fix it or we end it. Either she figures out why she's upset so much of the time and gets over it, or I'm out of here."

We spent the next several sessions exploring the destructive patterns in their marriage, especially those pertaining to their current crisis—both blaming the other for their anger. Both wanting to be treated with more love and consideration. I discovered that their marriage, like many others, was in critical condition and needed emergency repair.

Excruciating Pain

These couples aren't simply in pain. Their relationships are in acute crisis. Behind closed doors, they scream at one another, exchange destructive words, slam doors in anger, or spend their time together in silence. These couples don't survive because an emergency wasn't effectively managed and the couple wasn't prepared to handle the crisis.

Whether you're the one leaving, being left, or threatening to leave, marital crises are painful. If you've ever had a relationship fall apart, you know the anguish involved.

God meant for man and woman to live together in harmony for all time. Having created man, and seeing that he needed companionship, God said it wasn't good for him to be alone, so He created woman.

God undoubtedly knew that Adam and Eve would fall victim to

temptation, disobey Him, and reap many horrific consequences. Still, God's wish is for us to live in harmony. Adam said of Eve, "This is now bone of my bones and flesh of my flesh." We are literally bound together, and when we experience conflict that threatens our marriages, we're emotionally ripped apart.

Like physical symptoms telling us something is amiss in our bodies, marital distress says we're doing something wrong in our relationships. If we listen to these symptoms and respond to them effectively, we have the opportunity to save our marriages.

Common Warning Signs

Most people know when their marriage is in trouble. Although denial may provide temporary relief, it invariably breaks down, and couples eventually realize that something must be done.

Is that where you are today? Perhaps the denial has stopped working. You're in distress and need a marital miracle, but you're unsure where to turn. This book is an excellent place to begin.

Although you may have tried to convince yourself that the problems aren't that serious, you know better. You've become less sure about the stability and safety of your marriage. You know things are only going to get worse, but facing the truth is a frightening prospect.

Couples in crisis have a number of issues in common, including the following serious warning signs:

They experience ongoing conflict without any resolution of problems.

They become insensitive and demanding of each other.

They begin wishing for a new relationship.

They find excuses to spend more and more time away from each other.

They don't feel comfortable sharing personal feelings with each other.

They experience less and less physical intimacy.

They compare each other unfavorably to others.

Their relationship is filled with constant criticism and resentment.

They spread derogatory comments about each other.

They make or receive threats of separation or divorce.

Any of these symptoms is serious. In combination, they are even more threatening.

Fighting Without Resolution

Few things are as destructive as constant fighting. Although any amount of conflict takes its toll, fighting that involves verbal attacks, including sharp words or sarcasm, is especially deadly. Some couples avoid hurtful words and attack with distance instead. All of these behaviors erode the integrity of the marriage.

Perhaps you know couples who bicker about everything. They seem to find some perverse satisfaction in this kind of combat, which continues with no resolution in sight. I call these "round-robin fights" because they revisit the same issues again and again.

This type of endless battle is exhausting. The fighting focuses on people and not on solutions. These destructive habits cause people to lose respect for one another and lead to critical damage to their relationship.

Constant Criticism

Occasional criticism is hard enough to manage in a relationship. Constant criticism is a death blow. No one enjoys being criticized, and should this occur with any kind of frequency, a relationship will find itself in serious trouble. Criticism typically produces defensiveness and countercriticism. This leads to even more defensiveness, and the cycle continues.

John Gottman, in his book *Why Marriages Succeed or Fail,* describes this process:

> Criticism involves attacking someone's personality or character—rather than a specific behavior—usually with blame…Unlike complaints, criticisms tend to be generalizations. A telltale sign that you've slipped from complaining to criticizing is if global phrases like "you never" or "you always" start punctuating your exchanges.[1]

Gottman makes the point that complaining about a particular issue, provided you are focused on a specific topic and headed toward resolution, can actually be good for a marriage. However, couples who argue over generalities with no clear focus and who make no effort to solve problems find themselves in serious trouble.

Threats of Separation or Divorce

Nothing is quite like throwing out the explosive *D* word. Nothing causes your mate more anguish than making threats, especially about divorce or separation. Each of us needs stability and safety, and the spouse who uses these threats as weapons is employing a lethal strategy.

Unfortunately, such threats work only a time or two. After that, both partners are likely to start throwing the *D* bomb around like an overused four-letter word. One threat leads to other threats, which lead to increased resentment and hostility. The war escalates, and no one wins. The only guarantee is that the marriage will be in crisis.

Medic Alert

Just as the person experiencing acute medical distress needs special care, a couple in crisis also needs special treatment. When a person suffers from a severe medical condition, the medic or emergency room doctor doesn't spend hours gathering a comprehensive patient history. The medical personnel need specific information to stabilize the immediate situation. Long-range decisions can be made later. Long-range plans are irrelevant if the patient is dead.

The same analogy fits the marriage in crisis. The alert counselor doesn't approach the situation in the same way he or she approaches a longer-term counseling client. This is a time for immediate action that will accomplish several goals:

stabilize the marriage by decreasing conflict and increasing positive regard

assess the immediate emergency and set appropriate goals

prepare for longer-term work

provide encouragement and hope

At first glance, these may seem like very limited goals. However, if the clinician does not achieve them, there will be no patient to attend to in the weeks ahead. The patient, or in this case the marriage, will be DOA.

An Emergency Mind-Set

I write an advice column at Crosswalk.com, and every day my inbox is packed with urgent e-mails. The notes are filled with anguish as couples gasp for air, hoping beyond hope to find an answer that might save their marriage.

Because these situations are acute and so much is at stake, we must focus immediately on developing an urgent mind-set, just as an emergency room physician would have. Immediate action is needed, with a focused game plan and an eye toward healthy resolution. We hope for long-term outcomes, but we give our attention to the here and now.

Jake, an emergency medical technician I know, tells me that he and his crew are the first responders to many medical emergencies. As such, they have the power—in the absence of doctor's orders to the contrary—to perform nearly any action needed to stabilize patients until they reach the hospital, where additional staff will be standing by.

"This is life-or-death stuff, and we have to be alert, prepared, and ready for any kind of emergency. We know what we're looking for, what questions to ask, and what to do. Our job is to assess the problem and take immediate action."

We need this same mind-set when dealing with marital emergencies. Marriages in crisis are no less important than physical emergencies, and our actions and intentions need to be just as focused.

When a couple finally hits the bottom and confronts a crisis that could end their marriage, they're often willing to do *anything* to save their relationship.

But what exactly is an emergency mind-set? It includes these attitudes:

We will do whatever is needed to stabilize this marriage.

We will start doing those things immediately.

We will immediately stop doing those things that have created this crisis.

We will seek the level of help and intervention needed to save this marriage.

A Critical Moment

Every emergency, whether medical or marital, includes a critical moment when urgent action is essential. When the emergency alarm sounds, there's not a moment to spare.

Your marriage is at stake. This is a crisis—it is not a time to do what you've always done. It is not a time for business as usual. Real change requires real action!

You may be facing a critical moment in your marriage, and I am asking you to fully focus your attention on the advice in this book. Take nothing for granted. You have the power to manage this moment. How you approach it could mean ending the crisis or aggravating it. Attitude and focus are everything.

Intervention, Not Enabling

This book is about marriage lifesavers. It is about stopping the actions that have created the crisis in the first place. Two key terms will help you move through the steps necessary to heal your marriage.

The first critical term is *enabling,* which comes from the chemical dependency treatment field and refers to anything we do or don't do allowing a destructive process to continue.

Consider again Don and Brittany's marriage. It is interesting to note that they've been fighting destructively since the beginning. Don has always felt that Brittany fights unfairly, and she seems to have the same feelings about his tactics. Both complained about the other's surly attitude, sarcastic comments, and disrespect. Yet they enabled one another to continue in their destructive patterns. Only now, when both are sick and tired of feeling sick and tired, are they seeking change. Until now, they've enabled one another to keep doing what they've always done, so they've been getting what they've always gotten.

Imagine what could have happened if one of them had said to the other years ago, "It's time to stop doing this. We've got to make a change. We need professional help."

Consider some of the ways couples enable their relationships to flounder:

ignoring the problem
believing the problem will heal itself
continuing to act in the ways they've always acted
rationalizing their roles in the problem
minimizing the severity of the problem

These actions add to the emergency by enabling it and inhibiting you from working effectively on the issues that have created it. If you are going to be effective at emergency marriage repair, you must attack any tendency to enable the problem.

The opposite of *enabling* is our second key concept: *intervention.* An intervention is any effort you make to stop the destructive process. Any barrier you place in the path of the destructive process is an intervention. This includes any word you say or action you take that makes the destructive process less likely to continue.

That is what you're doing by picking up this book. By reading about marriages in crisis, by examining the things that can keep them there and the strategies that can change things for the better, you are moving in a positive direction that will yield positive results.

This book is about taking immediate action to stop the emotional hemorrhaging. An intervention includes these practical steps:

labeling the problem

acknowledging the severity and magnitude of the problem

owning our part in the problem

stopping our enabling behaviors

confronting the enabling behaviors in our mate

Picture EMTs in action. They are no-nonsense decision makers. They have no tolerance for anyone getting in the way. Interference is simply not allowed.

If you are going to make desired changes in your marriage, you must have the same urgent attitude. You must be like my EMT friend, who treats every call as a life-or-death matter.

You are undoubtedly reading this book because your marriage, or the marriage of someone you love, is in crisis. One critical step is to familiarize yourself with your actions that have enabled the destructive process. You must also determine to use only strategies that will create an intervention focused on salvaging the relationship.

Skillful Intervention

When you've reached this point, you cannot wait any longer. You need to determine who will assist you in this emergency. My suggestion is to select the best and brightest clinician you know. This is not the time to shop at the thrift store.

As a psychologist assisting couples through marital emergencies, my job is to give them every possible opportunity to save their relationship. Of course, I don't always succeed. However, when a couple comes to me with a spirit of humility and a willingness to recognize their part in the crisis, we often accomplish great things.

We must pull weeds (the destructive patterns of relating) and plant seeds (of healthy communication and conflict management) and pray for a little sunshine and rain. Doing these simple things can produce a bountiful crop in most cases.

As you face this time of crisis, it is essential to choose a seasoned clinician who is ready to lead the way. This is no time for a friend who will simply listen and empathize with your difficulties. You need a combat surgeon who's seen these crises before and is willing to take charge. You need someone to offer clear, incisive direction, so choose your interventionist wisely. A great deal is at stake.

Crisis or Opportunity

Although danger is a part of marital crisis, these times also bring incredible opportunity. I've been privileged on many occasions to assist couples through marital crises not only in my counseling practice but also in marriage intensives. These are always vulnerable, humbling, and powerful experiences. During three-day, ten-hour counseling sessions, I am able to fully get to know couples and help them discover their destructive patterns. I observe their nonverbal language, the way they approach each other, and the way they speak to each other.

I listen to how they solve their problems (or don't solve them). Do they find ways to create larger possibilities, or as so often happens, do they become ensnared in petty arguments and hurtful conversations? Once we outline the specific destructive patterns, we're in a much better position to end them.

Together with your counselor, you can find the destructive patterns and change them into effective interactions. You'll notice your marriage rebound as you free yourselves from the problems that have threatened your relationship.

If you're willing to learn new skills, you can make huge improvements. Your crisis can be an opportunity to shed damaging ways of relating and to exchange them for strategies that actually work.

Like a Child

Even though the situation is terribly serious, our work can be quite simple. All that is needed is for you to approach it with a child's heart.

Robert Fulgham, author of the bestseller *All I Really Need to Know I Learned in Kindergarten,* reminded us of life's basic truths. I quote his work often because I believe if we follow his advice, we'll be much happier.

Here are a few of his most valuable insights:

Share everything.

Play fair.

Put things back where you found them.

Clean up your own mess.

Don't take things that aren't yours.

Say you're sorry when you hurt somebody.

Wash your hands before you eat.

Flush.[2]

Although it might seem like a stretch to compare Robert Fulgham to Jesus, they said much the same thing, as can be seen in the following passage from the New Testament.

> Unless you change and become like little children, you will never enter the kingdom of heaven. Therefore, whoever humbles himself like this child is greatest in the kingdom of heaven (Matthew 18:3-4).

Notice that Jesus challenges us to *change*—suggesting that we move from knowing it all to being teachable. Jesus seems to note some urgency—the critical importance of change—but also simplicity in the process. As we work together and move from a state of emergency to a place of opportunity, I implore you to leave your ego at the door. With this attitude you'll discover what led to your crisis, find ways to stabilize your marriage, and be willing to change. This is the first step to repairing a damaged relationship.

2

Stabilizing Your Situation

I have come back again to where I belong; not an enchanted place, but the walls are strong.

Dorothy H. Rath

The sirens fade as the ambulance darts in and out of traffic on its way to the hospital. In the back of the emergency vehicle lies a frightened 80-year-old woman in excruciating pain. She has fallen and fractured her hip.

Amid the gasps of pain and anxiety, an uncertain calm and order settles in the back of the ambulance after an initial flurry of activity. The EMTs have been through crises like this countless times and are adept at taking charge during an emergency. They speak quiet words of reassurance as they administer medications to ease her pain. She is understandably anxious about her condition, but she responds positively to the EMTs' professional demeanor and their promises that she is in good hands and will be cared for.

The technicians are trained to offer hope, help, and stabilization during a crisis. They don't attend to every detail—only the immediate needs of the moment. The crisis demands that they limit their focus, and in doing so they provide an invaluable service.

Initially anxious, the woman begins to feel secure, knowing she is being cared for by trained professionals. She begins to relax, understanding that the EMTs are doing everything they can do at this moment. She must allow the hospital staff to do its work and trust the healing process.

For now, the situation has been stabilized and probably will not worsen.

This imagined scene offers a summary of our task. We too must sometimes work together in a controlled, detached manner to evaluate a crisis so we can quickly assess the extent of the damage and begin our focus on stabilizing your marriage. After we do this, we can broaden our scope of action.

I received a phone call yesterday from Mary, a panicky, tearful woman who had recently left her husband of three years. No longer able to put up with his angry shouting and name-calling, she left to stay with her girlfriend for the night.

"What happened, Mary?" I asked.

"I just can't take it anymore," she uttered between sobs. "He makes me crazy. I try to talk out our problems, but he turns everything around on me. It's always my fault, never his."

"But what happened that led to you leaving?" I asked.

She grew quiet as she tried to control her crying.

"He threatened to hit me," she said. "We were both yelling at each other. But he got really angry, cornered me, and threatened to slap me. I was scared for my life. I felt like I had to get out of the house. I don't know what to do now."

I had been working with Mary on the phone for several weeks and knew her marriage was unstable. "Let's slow things down and figure out what to do right now. You're in a crisis, and we need to handle first things first."

"He wants me to come back, but I'm afraid we'll just start arguing and fighting again. I've had all I can stand."

"Mary," I said, "you've separated from your husband for a reason. Things are not going well, and you've said you don't feel safe with him. I think you need to take a little time to reflect on your relationship. You need to think about what's not going well and about what needs to happen to change the destructive patterns. But you're not going to be able to do that while you're in the middle of this mess. Does that make sense?"

"Yes," she said. "But I already miss him, and I know he wants to see me. He says he's sorry for how he behaved."

"I'm sure that's true," I said. "But your marriage is in emergency mode. Your husband has been violent with you, and the two of you have been entrenched in bickering with each other for quite some time. You told me before that you can't take this kind of chaos anymore. Right?"

"He's driving me crazy," she admitted. "I know I shouldn't go back to him until we get some help."

"That's very wise," I said. "Let's let things cool down so that both of you have some space from the other. This will give you a chance to assess the problem. Then we can ascertain what kinds of changes need to take place. If you go back to him now, you'll ruin your chances for an effective intervention."

The Cooldown

During our next session, Mary let me know what happened after we finished our conversation.

It was dark and quiet that evening in her girlfriend's spare bedroom, and Mary wondered about her actions. She feared having made a mistake, one that would only make her husband angrier. With these thoughts flooding her mind, she felt confused and was unable to sleep.

Across town, her husband, Kyle, also lay awake, wondering about his marriage and worrying about his actions. In a later conversation with him I learned that he had spent the evening filled with regret and panic, and he had called their pastor, who spent several hours counseling with him. Kyle shared his history of violence and wondered aloud whether Mary would forgive him or end their marriage.

Mary too was reflective as she considered previous episodes of anger, when Kyle had threatened violence. She recalled the time he threw the phone across the room in a fit of rage. But she also thought about the times she had called him names, trying to hurt him as badly as he had hurt her. She knew they needed this time to cool down and consider their next course of action.

Learning how to effectively manage crisis is our goal. In some ways, the issue is not so much what we want to do as what we don't want to do. We need a time to cool down, to stabilize our current situation, so we can make rational decisions. We need peaceful time in a peaceful place, free from distraction, so we can put our marriage problems in perspective.

Panic is antithetical to rationality and stability. When thoughts and emotions are swirling within us like unruly children, making sound decisions is nearly impossible. With this chorus of questions and feelings clamoring for attention, we can easily slip back into primitive functioning—the fight-or-flight reaction. We tend either to attack a problem or to run from it. Both reactions are usually out of balance and unproductive.

Crisis emotions often lead to crisis moods. Each bad feeling or discouraging thought leads to another. Suddenly, a situation that once seemed manageable may feel completely out of control. Railing against these emotions only seems to muddy the waters.

Working Too Hard

Several weeks ago I began a therapy group for folks with eating disorders. I had been asked by numerous people to offer something to assist them in their struggle with obesity, bulimia, and other aspects of the disorder. Having worked in the field of addictions for years, and being a recovering workaholic myself, I decided to begin the group.

During the first several sessions, the members tenuously shared their stories. Filled with frustration over years of seemingly wasted efforts, they poured out their feelings. I listened and made a few comments as we got to know each other.

After the third meeting, I made a startling observation. The group members shared about their difficult struggle to combat their disorders, railing against themselves for being unable to conquer something that "shouldn't be this hard."

"Why do you say it shouldn't be this hard?" I asked one woman.

"Well," she said, hardly pausing, "it's simple. I know exactly what to do, and I should be able to do it. I've read dozens of books on dieting, healthy eating, and exercise. You name the book, I've got it. Losing weight just shouldn't be this hard."

"Do the rest of you agree?" I asked the other members, each wondering where I was going with this question.

"Yes, and no," a man answered. "I agree that it shouldn't be this hard, but I've been fighting this problem for thirty years, so evidently it really *is* this hard."

We spent the balance of that session and the next talking about the power of addictions, the limits of our flesh nature, and the need to go easy on ourselves. We have to take active steps to understand and work on our addiction, but we must be careful not to shame ourselves.

"In some ways you're working too hard," I said cautiously. "You berate yourselves, look for quick fixes, and then sabotage your efforts. You must learn how to work on these problems more effectively. That's the answer."

I watched as each member sighed and noticeably relaxed. They didn't have to work so hard—just more effectively. It wasn't all up to them—they had me, the group, and God to help them. They were no longer alone with their secrets.

Gaining Perspective

Mary and others dealing with marriage emergencies need to allow their emotions and situations to simmer in order to gain a fresh perspective. They need to stop trying to fix things immediately and to take time for reflection.

In the midst of conflict, we can easily develop tunnel vision. We see things one way and then rehearse that perspective, determining not to entertain any other. Unfortunately, many people never realize when they've limited their vision. Only when they step back can they see how narrowly they're viewing things.

Tunnel vision comes on insidiously rather than all at once. It often occurs over a long period of time as we develop a certain attitude and then adopt beliefs that support a particular point of view. Unfortunately, as we solidify that view, we also limit our ability to take in new information. Consider the impact of tunnel vision:

We slowly relinquish our broad perspective.

We create barriers between ourselves and others.

We limit the amount of new input we're willing to receive.

We shrink and destabilize our world.

We pit our point of view against others'.

You can see how tunnel vision is one product of an unstable relationship and how it creates further instability. Positive marital health requires that we remain open to new information. Stepping back and gaining perspective can reduce tunnel vision and restabilize a relationship.

Additionally, as we calm down, we may discover that what we thought was the problem is not the actual issue at all. As we reflect and consider, we develop a broader perspective, which helps us learn why something bothers us so much. The current dispute may lead us to the root of the problem.

Stabilizing Tactics

Reeling from instability in your marriage, you may lose sight of what you can do to stabilize your relationship and end the crisis. In times of confusion and chaos, it's helpful to have a recipe for stabilization—a clear road map to keep things from spiraling out of control. Consider some of these practical steps:

1. Take a time-out. We must first remove ourselves from the urgent problem. We need space and time to clear our heads. By doing so, we give ourselves an opportunity to reflect on the way we've been acting

and the impact the current crisis is having on our lives. By slowing things down and cooling down, we give ourselves and our mate a chance to change direction. In a time-out, we put the relating part of the relationship on hold.

What might this look like? Many crises require a separation of a few feet or a few miles. You and your mate may agree to go to separate corners of the house until things settle down. You might create a literal separation, such as a trial separation, as was the case for Mary. This may occur as the result of a catastrophic outburst or as the result of months of deliberation. A trial therapeutic separation can give you the opportunity to consider your situation.

It might also simply be a truce, where you agree to put your hot issues into an imaginary container, put it on the shelf, and take it down in front of your pastor or marriage counselor. In the safety of the counseling relationship, you can explore the issues more effectively.

2. Neutralize defenses. Almost anything you say during a marital crisis can generate defensiveness. Therefore, you would both do well to agree to closely monitor defensive responses. Be exceedingly cautious about saying things in an accusatory or critical manner. Likewise, be careful to own your feelings, taking responsibility for your actions and reactions. You will be tempted to overreact emotionally. When this happens, small skirmishes can escalate into major battles. Agree to be very loving and careful with one another.

3. Talk about certain topics with special care and boundaries. Emergencies demand that we act differently. You and your spouse need to agree that if you are going to talk about hot topics, you will do so in the most cautious manner possible. You agree to set time limits on certain topics so that anyone who feels threatened can halt the discussion.

4. Agree to disagree. Not all issues require immediate solutions. In fact, some of them may never be solved. For that reason, you both need to find a way to live in harmony during this challenging time. Don't try to hammer out a solution to every problem. Be willing to look at one another and simply note that you don't see eye to eye.

By agreeing to disagree, you can eliminate power struggles. If you attack every problem and strive to solve every issue, you'll find yourself pressuring your partner to think the way you think. Don't do it. Allow for differences. This strategy will breathe new life into your marriage.

5. Treat each other with respect. This strategy will take willpower, good intentions, and a humble spirit. You'll need a heart bathed in prayer so you can treat your mate lovingly in spite of negative feelings.

But what about all that anger and resentment? What do you do with that?

You compartmentalize it, taking it off the shelf only at agreed upon times in agreed upon places. This skill, called *conflict containment,* is used specifically for putting an issue aside until you can talk about it in an evenhanded way. You understand that to do otherwise might sabotage your marriage. In spite of the bad feelings you harbor for your mate, you recognize that you still have an obligation, and hopefully a desire, to treat your mate with respect.

6. Listen to and be willing to be influenced by your mate. Perhaps the biggest step you can take toward gaining a new perspective and stabilizing your relationship is to truly listen to your partner. What has he or she been trying to say to you that you've been unwilling to hear? In what ways has tunnel vision kept you from broadening your point of view? I'm not saying this marriage crisis is entirely your fault—but you can help stabilize things by broadening your point of view, and you can accomplish this by listening to your mate.

In addition to listening to your mate, it is important to let his or her words influence you. Just as you let your inner wisdom soak in and just as you allow the wisdom of God to settle into your bones, allow your mate's perspective to settle in as well. Reflect on what your partner has been saying to you. The message probably is not a new one; perhaps he or she has been trying to share it for some time.

Willingness to Change

The best place to mold character, the best "love chemistry laboratory," is a marriage. In your marriage you are vulnerable and transparent. No one knows you like your mate knows you. He or she sees the good and the bad. During these challenging times, you can stabilize your marriage by being willing to change. In addition to listening, reassure your mate that you have heard and understood the message, and then take it one step further—practice change.

Before you begin protesting that your partner needs to change just as much as you, note that I'm not talking about anyone but you. Your partner is responsible for his or her stuff, and you're responsible for yours. Understanding the difference is critical.

But you've been treated unfairly, you say. Yes, and that's something for him or her to deal with.

But your mate has character issues too, you insist. Yes, and again, that's your mate's stuff to deal with.

You never have to own more than your stuff. You have the right to set limits on how much you hear at any given time. But if you stop protesting and start listening, you will have done a great deal to stabilize things. Ask yourself these questions:

What are the concerns that keep being conveyed to me in one form or another?

What have I felt convicted about that needs to change?

What are the issues I've always wanted to change within myself?

A willingness to change is perhaps one of the most loving things you can bring to a marriage. When your mate sees that you are willing to change, you will likely be met with a reciprocal attitude of graciousness. When we feel loved, we feel a freedom to risk changing. Likewise, your attitude will help your mate feel free to risk changing.

The 12-step program made famous by Alcoholics Anonymous asks members to subscribe to three principles:

Honesty—to face yourself as honestly as possible, being willing to look beyond natural defenses to see the character traits in need of change.

Openness—to be open to feedback from the group and to inspect your life in light of that feedback.

Willingness—to allow yourself to be changed by God, the group, and others.

Honesty, openness, and willingness are powerful tools. When we take the focus off our mate and inspect our own inner attitudes and behaviors, relational conflict lessens. Honesty, openness, and willingness become principles that guide our daily lives, not only in times of crisis but also in good times.

Humor

Another stabilizing strategy deserves a section all its own—the use of humor. If you're reading this book during a time of marital crisis, you've probably lost the art of using humor in your relationship. The bad times outweigh the good, and seriousness has suffocated the humor. This needs to change.

Recently, an older couple came to see me about a longstanding difference that was causing problems in their marriage. The wife had a habit of retreating whenever she felt any tension in the relationship. This was particularly frustrating for her husband because he hated leaving issues unresolved.

During the counseling sessions, we explored her history of avoiding conflict and retreating whenever it arose. She shared that she had grown up with constant tension because of an alcoholic father. He had grown up in a family where issues were always resolved and never left to simmer.

When they arrived at one session, the couple was clearly very happy. When they walked into my office, I asked what had happened to make them so cheerful.

"We created a new game," she said. "Whenever we're really angry with one another and locked in a power struggle, instead of retreating, we agreed to talk using only sign language and sounds."

"Huh?" I said.

He then demonstrated. Gesturing and waving his arms wildly, he made grunting sounds.

In response, she crossed her arms, and shouted, "Pffft!"

Both began laughing uncontrollably.

"It's worked great," she said. "Neither one of us can keep it up for very long before we realize how ridiculous our argument is. It really breaks the tension."

I've since recommended this strategy to other couples with wonderful results. Yes, it's a silly game and likely to make you feel a bit childish. But that's the point. Rather than staying locked in a dreadful situation, how about combating the situation with a little levity?

We should not be surprised by the stabilizing impact of humor. Solomon noted as much: "A cheerful heart is good medicine, but a crushed spirit dries up the bones" (Proverbs 17:22).

In his book *Anatomy of an Illness,* Norman Cousins writes of being diagnosed with a crippling and extremely painful disc degeneration of his spine. When traditional medicine failed, he decided to try alternative medicine—humor. With many sleepless nights, Dr. Cousins adopted a regimen of Marx Brothers films and *Candid Camera* classics. Ten minutes of daily belly laughter gave him at least two hours of pain-free sleep every evening.

How can this technique be a lifesaver for your marriage? Look for ways to infuse humor into your daily life. Discover ways to find the humor in a crisis. Agree to poke a bit of fun at your situation as a way to help stabilize a marital crisis.

Rules of Engagement

During times of marital crises and during times of peace, couples need rules of engagement. I can think of no better stabilizing force than the application of perhaps my favorite verse in the New Testament, written by the apostle Paul. Speaking to the church at Ephesus, which had been struggling with conflict in the ranks, he says, "Do not let any unwholesome talk come out of your mouths, but only what is helpful for building others up according to their needs, that it may benefit those who listen" (Ephesians 4:29).

The apostle Paul shows us that our words have the power to destabilize or stabilize. They have the power to build others up or tear them down. They have the power to instruct us or create conflict and tension.

What have you done with words in your marriage? Do your words show you to be kind, or are you critical and reactive?

Consider the challenge of using your words to build up your mate *according to his or her needs.* As Paul noted, it is not enough to speak positively to your partner—your words must also build up your partner according to his or her needs at the time.

Am I suggesting that we're supposed to have some inkling as to our mate's needs? Yes. And are we supposed to be so unselfish that we tune into our mate's needs even while we struggle with anger and animosity? Again, yes. This is most challenging, but it is our calling. And it produces a bountiful harvest.

Few things are as life changing and energy giving as being ministered to according to our needs. When someone speaks into our lives at our very point of need, we are encouraged and strengthened. This is a strong and dynamic way of stabilizing your marriage.

The Eye of the Storm

I was raised in a boating family, and my father had "two-foot-itis," that incurable condition that left him constantly desiring a larger boat. As a result, he increased his boat's size by two feet or more every couple of years.

Because I grew up near salt water, and because my father longed to be on the water at every possible opportunity, I've also developed a love for sailing. I've experienced nearly every boating calamity short of capsizing. I've been in surging tides that pushed and pulled our boat in every direction. I've ridden out storms with waves that crashed mercilessly against our boat. On my father's wall is a tapestry made by my sister that reads, "Dear God, protect me. The ocean is so big, and my boat is so small."

This must have been the way the disciples felt when they faced a horrendous storm on the Sea of Galilee. They floundered about like a matchstick on the waves while Jesus slept.

The disciples were experienced fishermen, accustomed to the sudden storms that erupted on this large body of water. Yet in spite of their experience, they panicked when confronted by a furious storm.

In distress, they awakened Jesus: "Lord, save us! We're going to drown!"

They knew the ferocity of the wind and waves and felt powerless to find safety and stability in the storm.

Jesus seemed less than sympathetic to their plight. " 'You of little faith, why are you so afraid?' Then he got up and rebuked the winds and waves, and it was completely calm" (Matthew 8:25-26).

The disciples' anxiety is understandable. It was, after all, "a furious storm." However, Jesus goes right to the heart of the issue—their lack of faith. Faith in this instance would have calmed their anxious hearts with assurance that the Master of the winds and waves was right beside them.

Today, as you read these words, you may be experiencing the storm of your life. You may be floundering in your tiny boat. In fact, with emotions spiraling out of control, you may feel much like the disciples, completely at the mercy of forces outside yourself.

If this describes your situation, your faith can be an authoritative influence. Faith delivers you from unruly forces. While the waves rage outside, your faith can stabilize you inside. God promises to hear your pleas for help and to respond. He promises to offer wisdom and to empower you to eliminate behaviors that led to the crisis.

You don't have to manage every aspect of the problem. Like the woman in the back of the ambulance who trusted the medic, and like the disciples who needed to practice trusting the Master of the wind and waves, you can let your faith have a strong, stabilizing impact on your marriage crisis.

3

Creating Safety

Never does the human soul appear so strong as when it foregoes revenge and dares to forgive an injury.

E.H. Chapin

Having just graduated from high school, I looked forward to a lazy summer before heading north to Canada and Covenant Bible School. My mind was on crabbing on Puget Sound, water skiing on Lake Whatcom, and seeing if my buddies and I could fit that 327-cubic-inch engine into my '55 Chevrolet.

I had always been healthy and energetic, so I was shocked and frightened when what appeared to be a common cold turned into something far more serious. I wasn't sneezing or sniffling, but my painful wheezing wouldn't go away.

My parents were equally concerned. My mother boiled water and had me stand over the steam for hours in an attempt to loosen the congestion and ease my panic. It didn't work. I simply couldn't breathe. My chest felt like it was in a vice, allowing only shallow breaths of air to enter my lungs. The more I fought for breath, the more frightened I became.

There was no choice now but to call the doctor, who suggested lathering me with Vicks VapoRub and purchasing a vaporizer. It soon became apparent that these interventions were too little too late.

Fatigued from my struggle, after several hours of wheezing and gasping for air, I begged my parents to take me to the hospital. Out of breath and exhausted from the ordeal, I wanted help. I wanted to breathe. I wanted the safety that comes from knowing the situation was under control and I was being cared for.

We climbed into the family station wagon and headed for St. Luke's Hospital in our hometown of Bellingham, Washington. My mother assured me that the doctors would be waiting and that they would have the answers. I'd always feared hospitals, but now I looked forward to the quiet hallways and the sterile smell of antiseptic and chlorine. No longer was I afraid of the sick people lying in beds waiting for help. I wanted that help too.

When we arrived at the emergency room, a nurse immediately assisted us. She asked questions about my condition and assured us that things would be okay. The emergency was over, she said. I was safe.

Maybe this is how couples feel when they meet with a trusted counselor when their relationship is in shambles. In an emergency, we need stability and safety—we must know that things are not likely to get worse and that more often than not, they will get better with proper treatment.

Safety Defined

I've repeatedly used medical crises as a way to understand marital crises; I believe they have similar qualities. My medical problems were mediated by kind, loving parents and the physicians who cured me. And I was offered a safe place where I could wrestle with my illness.

This book offers you a similar place of sanctuary. Safety in a relationship means having an agreement not to harm one another in any way. You feel free to be exactly who you are, think exactly what you think, and feel what you feel. Safety within a marriage is not an add-on or an optional bonus feature. It's integral to your relationship, and without it your marriage will ultimately dissolve.

Take a moment to consider the current state of your relationship. Can you and your mate…

share your thoughts without fear of criticism?

know you will not be judged for your feelings?

disagree without condemnation?

know you'll never be threatened or intimidated?

know you'll never be subjected to excessive control?

This is a time to be brutally honest and to face the situation the way it is, not the way you'd like it to be. Your answers will offer important information about the safety of your marriage. Remember, creating safety is not optional—it is imperative. This chapter involves strategies for creating safety as you seek to stabilize your marriage crisis and move into healing.

Vowing never to harm your mate and never to allow yourself to be harmed by your mate may seem like a tall order if you're experiencing volatile emotions. After all, to reach a marriage crisis, specific actions by you, your mate, or both of you have undoubtedly contributed to a decrease in stability and safety. In this case, intent is everything. We will discuss the specific ways you create or experience a lack of safety, and of course ways to generate it, but first we must begin with intent—a commitment not to harm or coerce your mate in any way.

An Unsafe Marriage

Recently, I worked with a couple hanging on to the last vestiges of their relationship. Their disdain for one another was obvious, and they were considering divorce.

Zane and Marsha were 55 and 53, respectively, and both had been married previously. In their tenth year of marriage, they now faced a crisis. Zane was a portly man, weighing nearly 300 pounds, but he was dressed impeccably, with a buttoned-down, pin-striped shirt and pressed khakis. I learned that Marsha, a slight, attractive woman who dressed years younger than her age in a short, tight-fitting skirt, took an active interest in buying him clothes.

Normally, I'd consider this to be a healthy sign for a marriage, but in this case Marsha made it clear that she bought clothes for Zane because, as she said, "He'd look like a tramp if I didn't dress him." During the first session, she made frequent offhand attacks on his character. Hostility dripped from her in the form of nitpicky criticisms.

"Please tell me why you've come in for counseling," I said. "What are you hoping to accomplish?"

Marsha wasted no time in getting to the point.

"He cares more about his business than he does me," Marsha said angrily. "I can't get him to show me even the slightest bit of interest. I talk, and he stares at the television or out the window."

"Oh, c'mon," Zane shouted. "I'm here, aren't I?"

"And you dragged your feet the whole way."

"That's not true," he said.

"So, what exactly is the problem?" I said.

"I'm just here to be the dutiful, loving husband," Zane replied sarcastically.

"Yep, you're the best," Marsha said. "Go ahead. Make it look like you're trying to please me."

I could see during the first few moments that this couple had already reached the later stages of marriage disturbance Dr. John Gottman describes in his book *Why Marriages Fail.*

Zane seemed somewhat indifferent to his wife's barbs and continued to smile and joke in an apparent attempt to distract her. He acted oblivious to their obvious crisis.

"She's a high-maintenance woman, Doc. I've worked hard to get her the house she wants and to furnish it right. But she wants more communication, and I know I've got to work on that."

"Oh, please," Marsha said, stringing out the words for effect. "If you wanted to communicate more with me, you'd throw that stupid plasma television in the dumpster and turn off your cell phone at night. Our marriage is on its last legs, but you don't want to change."

"Nothing I do is good enough for you," Zane said, now appearing discouraged.

"Let's take a breath and reflect on why you're here," I said. "You two are clearly in trouble, and we've got to get to the heart of the matter quickly to stabilize your marriage. I hear a lot of things being said, but I'm not sure what the real issue is."

I took an extra moment to study this couple, who were obviously in so much pain.

"Marsha, our intake sheet says you've been married for ten years. Have you folks struggled with communication for all ten years?"

"All ten!" Marsha said. "Here we are, still not talking after all these years. I can't take it any longer. This is no marriage."

"I try to be available as much as work allows," Zane said. "But I've got to make money while I can, and besides"—he paused, considering his next words—"she wants the vacation house and the Audi wagon, and those things don't come cheap."

"I can't believe you said that," she sputtered. "I'd gladly give up those things to have you emotionally present."

Zane laughed.

"What's so funny?" Marsha asked. "You know it's the truth."

"Let's get real, Marsha. You love your things too much to give them up."

For the remainder of the session, Zane tried unsuccessfully to dissuade Marsha from her anger. Marsha's resentment leaked into her every word as she strongly hinted that she was nearly finished with the marriage.

Zane reiterated that he felt as if he could not do anything to please Marsha, and she said that nothing would change until she got more attention from him. Her approach made him bristle, and his rejection made her recoil in anger. If something didn't change, they were surely headed for divorce.

Near the end of the session, I tried to be as direct as possible about their situation.

"Folks," I said, "I've got some news for you that I'd think should be obvious. Your marriage is in serious trouble. You must take immediate action to stabilize the situation and create safety. If we aren't successful at that, I'm predicting that the marriage won't last another year."

Both nodded in agreement and affirmed that they wanted to work on their marriage but that they were very frustrated with one another.

"It's natural to be tired and frustrated," I told them. "I don't expect either of you to want to dive into working on things when you're so angry. Our first task is simply to create safety—a space free from attacks, free from barbs and sarcasm. We have to declare a neutral zone, where you can both breathe and collect yourself. This will create safety, and then we can work on a deeper level."

"I'm all for that," Marsha said firmly.

"Sounds good," Zane said, nodding.

Safety Violated

Zane and Marsha were in crisis mode, though like many couples, they attempted to hide their instability. However, they knew that even a strong faith and sturdy moral principles were not enough to keep them together if they continued to harm each other. In time, under enough pressure, every marriage buckles from the strain.

Most couples don't use language about stability and safety. In fact, they rarely think about it. Because of that, they hardly notice when they behave in ways that violate marriage's essential principles.

Were you to walk in the door tonight and tell your mate that you don't feel safe in your relationship, you'd probably get the same response as if you had three eyes. That's partly what makes this book unique. You'll learn about creating stability and safety, and you'll make strides toward creating an atmosphere that will help you heal the wounds that have brought you to this broken place.

Although you might think a marital relationship would be the safest place on earth, couples violate each other's safe places on a daily basis. Ultimately, these violations rip at the core of the marriage. In fact, couples violate one another so frequently, they hardly give a second thought to these harmful behaviors.

Our goal is to bring that behavior to a screeching halt.

It's time you gained clarity about the boundary violations that lead to marriage crises. It's time you learned about the language of stability and safety and about the behaviors that help and the behaviors that hinder.

Blame

During this acrimonious time in your marriage, you may be more tempted than ever to blame your mate. After all, you tell yourself, he's blaming you, so why not blame him? That's why blame is the primary ingredient in the problems experienced by couples in crisis.

It simply doesn't work. Blame never heals. It never solves problems. Blame does only one thing—it creates defensiveness and animosity toward your mate.

Consider the purpose of blame: to affix responsibility onto another person. Invariably, when a couple in crisis seeks my services, they're entrenched in a complex pattern of Who Dunnit? Like sleuths in an old episode of *Columbo* or an Agatha Christie murder mystery, they are eager to point the finger of blame.

"If it weren't for you, we'd be fine," she says.

"Yeah," he retorts, "and if it weren't for you, all my problems would disappear."

She sees his weaknesses and relishes pointing them out, saying, "It's all your fault."

Each responds by dodging the shame and blame. But what neither sees is that pointing the finger only makes them angrier and angrier at one another, which escalates the crisis.

Are you a blamer? Do you and your mate point fingers at one another, or are you problem solvers, taking responsibility for the issues you bring to your marriage?

Shame

Another devastating aspect of blame, especially for a marriage in crisis, is the shame that is closely connected to blaming. Shaming comments indicate not only that you have done something wrong but also that you are bad to the bone.

Shame is conveyed not only in words, such as "I can't believe you did that," or "How could you do such a thing?" but also through voice tone, gestures, and expressions.

Consider the destructive power of these weapons:

sneers

sarcastic comments

rolled eyes

smacked lips

furrowed brows

Each act conveys something incredibly powerful and destructive. Shame can leave you feeling stupid, worthless, and even ridiculous.

You can see how shame tears down and destroys, builds barriers, undermines self-esteem, and causes pain. It can bring devastation to couples trying to rebuild their relationship, so it must be considered completely off-limits.

Criticism

Criticism is closely related to blame, but whereas blaming involves transferring responsibility for problems to your mate, criticism involves noticing every annoying thing your mate does. Another term for it is *nit-picking.*

Criticism in marriage is like a computer virus, infecting every aspect of your marriage and slowing interactions to a crawl. Many couples seem oblivious to their use of criticism, and soon both partners are sharing their dissatisfaction with the other about insignificant issues. As with blame, criticism serves only to create defensiveness, hostility, and a lack of safety.

The apostle Paul was quite familiar with the effects of criticism. He was soundly criticized at times, and he also challenged believers to eradicate criticism from the church. Consider his words:

> I urge you to live a life worthy of the calling you have received. Be completely humble and gentle; be patient, bearing with one another in love. Make every effort to keep the unity of the Spirit through the bond of peace (Ephesians 4:1-3).

If you're in a marital crisis, criticism can become malignant, invading every part of your relationship and eradicating safety. Consider evaluating the extent to which you've allowed criticism into your marriage. Once you've done this, accept the challenge to "bear with one another in love" and to seek peace with your partner.

Mind Reading

Boundaries commonly become fuzzy in a marriage or close relationship. This happens when one person believes she knows what the other person is thinking, feeling, or intending.

Consider the following dialogue between Marsha and Zane:

"He doesn't really care about our marriage," Marsha said. "All he thinks about is his work."

This is a perfect example of mind reading. Marsha told me what Zane was thinking and what he cared about. Although she might be right, making such an assertion violates his boundaries and is sure to bring a defensive response.

But Zane seemed capable of mind reading as well.

"You want more than I can afford," he told Marsha. "That's why I have to work so much. You value your things more than you value me."

Again, he might be right in his suspicions, but to make this assertion is to say something only Marsha has the right to say.

Can you see how these tactics are sure to destroy the safety in a relationship? Generally, if one partner practices mind reading, the other is going to be reluctant to share personal information.

Controlling Behavior

People don't feel safe when others try to control their thoughts, feelings, or actions. In fact, such behavior is a form of violence. Intimacy cannot survive in this atmosphere.

Again, let's consider Marsha and Zane's situation.

Marsha wants Zane to enter more fully into their marriage. Although we may sympathize with her desire to have him limit his hours at work, we cannot support the way she talks to him. Martha must be careful not to coerce Zane into thinking the way she thinks or behaving the way she'd like him to behave. She'll log much more mileage if, rather than being critical, she lovingly invites him into a greater level of intimacy by asking specifically—and politely—for what she needs.

One of the surest paths to marital crises is to attempt to control your mate. Although it is natural to want your mate to think, feel, and behave in ways that are consistent with your values, you cannot make that happen. Couples must give each other the freedom to express their individuality. Hopefully, if they have chosen each other carefully, their values will coincide.

One of the most common reactions to controlling behavior is rebellion. Undoubtedly you've seen this destructive process at work. The more we try to force people into thinking the way we think or doing what we want them to do, the greater the likelihood they will rebel. This is a natural response.

A far more effective approach is to allow your mate to be different from you and to invite him or her into a cooperative relationship where you both can explore creative agreements and win-win solutions.

Forecasting Doubt

Marriage is a delicate thing and must be treated carefully. It is the place where we are allowed to try on new ideas and behaviors. It is like a cocoon of safety for the emerging butterfly.

One of the greatest strengths in my marriage is that my wife believes in my ideas. Although she exercises the freedom to express doubt if they are off the wall, for the most part I know she will express encouragement, thereby creating safety for me to talk about whatever is on my mind. I try to extend the same courtesy and respect to her.

Safety is built on pillars of trust and encouragement. When we trust our mate and believe in his or her ability to handle situations, we've done a great deal to create safety. On the other hand, when we project doubt and distrust, we broadcast a different message: "This relationship is not safe for you. I'm going to attack and discourage your ideas."

But what if a couple genuinely doesn't believe in what each other is saying or doesn't agree with their ideas? Doesn't a marriage have room for honest feedback without shame, sarcasm, or ridicule?

Keep in mind that if your marriage is in crisis, you are more delicate and vulnerable than at other times. That's why a huge dose of TLC and encouragement is critical to strengthening the marriage. In his book *His Needs, Her Needs,* Willard Harley taught us the importance of what he referred to as "love banks": "Each person either makes deposits or withdrawals whenever we interact with him or her. Pleasurable interactions cause deposits, and painful interactions cause withdrawals."[1]

That's simple enough. However, you might be asking if Harley is saying that we must watch everything we say, always paying attention to our account with our mate?

Yes.

Every interaction in your marriage leaves you feeling positive or negative about each other and about your marriage. Although no single incident is likely to cause you to be overdrawn on your love bank, repeated withdrawals will certainly do so. Marriages with accounts that are constantly overdrawn are soon in a state of emergency.

Labeling and Name-Calling

You and your spouse are responsible for creating an environment where love can thrive. This cannot take place in an atmosphere where name-calling or labeling is commonplace. A marriage crisis simply leaves no room for put-downs.

Recently, I worked with a man who sought out my services to help his wife, who had been diagnosed with borderline personality disorder. During one of our counseling sessions, he made the following remark to her:

"Honey, you know you overreact to things and that you are far too emotional. I'm just trying to help you see the big picture and keep things in perspective."

I watched the wife wince at his words even though he talked in a very loving voice. He was surprised when she practically jumped out of her chair to confront him.

"I don't like being called the sick one, and I don't like it when you use that fatherly voice to put me down."

Her reaction caught me off guard, and I had to take a moment to explore what had happened. As I reflected on their conversation, I could see how he had labeled her. She became defensive and did a good job of setting a healthy boundary. He understood the problem with his label and vowed not to do it again.

Many couples are not so subtle in labeling one another. When angry, they commonly point out each other's deficiencies, labeling them as bad or wrong. Such shame-based comments invariably erode the safety in a marriage.

Deception

Healthy marriages are built on honesty. Even the tiniest deception can bring down the relational house.

Couples in crisis commonly struggle with honesty. Lacking trust and safety with one another, they begin hiding their true feelings. In my experience, they are often deceptive about one or more of these things:

money matters
sexual issues

hidden concerns

feelings

differing beliefs

Unfortunately, deception often occurs in a climate where one partner feels unsafe. If you fear being criticized for your actions or thoughts, you will likely hold back the truth from your mate. However, in doing so, you add to the relational problem because your deception will make your mate feel unsafe as well. Safety to express everything, even unpleasant matters, must be a foundational element in every marriage.

As you consider your current marital situation, take a moment to discern the level of honesty in your relationship. Has deception played a role in the crises you've been through? If so, consider what actions will make your marriage a safe place to share your problems and concerns.

Creating Safety

Safety is far more than the presence or absence of certain behaviors. Every couple must make safety a part of their relationship. This is even more critical for the couple experiencing an emergency in their marriage, largely because events and circumstances have created a lack of safety.

We all need safety in order to learn and grow, to open our hearts, to be vulnerable, and to risk loving. We've all seen safety vanish in a flash when someone has been judgmental, used harsh words, or criticized us unnecessarily. We've also experienced the joy that comes with being treated with love and compassion.

Consider some of the qualities needed to create safety in marriage:

- Both people take responsibility for their feelings and behaviors. The key ingredient here is that they don't blame each other.
- Both people protect each other, never intentionally

violating or harming each other. In a caring, loving relationship, they both make the effort to protect and honor their mate.

- Both people remain open to learning about themselves and their mate. In a safe relationship, each partner listens to the other and provides feedback that will help the other grow.
- Both people set inner and outer boundaries that their mate respects. Knowing they cannot read minds, they respect their mate's unique thoughts and perspective. They don't try to dissuade each other from their opinions. Likewise, they honor their own boundaries and encourage their mate to honor them as well.
- Each person guards against abusive behaviors, such as yelling, name-calling, smothering, or demanding. Both people understand that these behaviors sabotage safety and can cause irreparable damage.
- Each person practices telling the truth in loving ways. Understanding the importance of keeping the slate clean, they inform each other about their feelings, thoughts, and desires. They practice vulnerability, knowing this brings them closer to each other and creates safety.

We are tempted to focus on protecting ourselves, but this usually results in an absence of safety. When we are afraid to share our truth or we resist learning about our mate, safety dies and takes love down with it.

Recently, I worked with Tom and Denell, who had separated after months of constant conflict. Their years of struggle had come to a particularly painful and emergent point.

At a session not long ago, each showed the discomfort of their current struggle—how they might attend their son's graduation from high school, an event they wanted to celebrate as a family but that was made more difficult by their recent separation.

An animated woman prone to dramatic outbursts, Denell leaned forward and spoke forcefully to Tom, a slender man who appeared frozen in his chair.

"I've been afraid of you during this past year, Tom," she stated. "I'm not saying it's all been your fault. I've contributed to our problems. But I'm learning about boundaries, and I'm only going to Tad's graduation with you if I can feel safe with you. I don't want to fight or discuss anything heated at his graduation. If I can't feel safe about this, we're not going together."

"I can do that," Tom said.

"I need you to understand what safety looks like for me, and then you can tell me what it looks like for you."

Tom stared at Denell, and though he may not have listened carefully in the months leading to their separation, he listened intently now.

She had obviously prepared for this session. Looking down at a piece of paper she had pulled from her purse, she read the following items:

"I don't want you to lose your temper with me in any way. If you get angry, I'm going to ask you to leave.

"Don't be gruff or surly with me.

"If I feel threatened by what you're saying, I'll ask you to stop. If you don't, I'll ask you to leave and sit somewhere else.

"If you won't leave when I ask, I'll get up and leave. If you follow me, I'll call the police. I need to know you'll absolutely honor my boundaries. Things need to be predictable for me. I need to know that I'm in control of how I feel and how things will go. I don't want any surprises."

"What do you think of Denell's request, Tom?" I asked.

"It's reasonable, and I think I can do it."

"Do you have any requests of your own?"

Tom thought for a moment and then shook his head. Dabbing at his eyes, he looked at Denell and apologized.

"I'm sorry for making you feel unsafe," he said. "I've got a lot to learn, and I'm willing to learn it. I want you to feel safe in our marriage. It's never been my intent to hurt you. I'm willing to work very hard on everything you've asked for."

"That would be great, Tom, and I'll do the same for you," Denell said warmly.

Denell and Tom were able to attend their son's high school graduation together without conflict. They'd outlined exactly what they needed, and because they still felt love for one another, they worked hard to offer safety to each other. Although they remain separated, Tom and Denell are working hard to restore safety to their marriage. Because of that, their crisis is beginning to stabilize.

A Disarming Approach

We shouldn't be surprised that Jesus had a unique way of creating safety in His relationships. Time and again we read stories in the Gospels where Jesus sits with and teaches His friends and disciples. They want to hear what He has to say to them.

At other times, Jesus uses various situations as teachable moments. Perhaps you've had those with your children or a friend. Circumstances are such that you are able to speak into their life and provide guidance.

Such was the case on the road to Samaria. Tired from His journey, Jesus asked the Samaritan woman to give Him a drink. Since He was a Jew, she wondered why He would ask her for a drink. However, in doing so, Jesus broke the ice and established contact.

Having been given a drink and showing her that He had no need to establish superiority, He begins discussing deeper things.

"If you knew the gift of God and who it is that asks you for a drink, you would have asked him and he would have given you living water" (John 4:10). They initially talked about the superficialities of obtaining water, but they were soon having an intimate conversation—one that she certainly would not have participated in if she had not felt safe.

I can picture Jesus and this woman sipping water on a hot, sultry day. Initially feeling uncomfortable and embarrassed, she begins discussing her life. Jesus tells her that she's had five husbands, and the man she's currently living with is not her husband. He doesn't judge or condemn her, but He encourages her to change her life and to develop a personal relationship with God. Here, beside a well, on a dusty, country road, we are shown how safety creates openness, relationship, and healing.

4

Establishing Trust

It is impossible to go through life without trust: That is to be imprisoned in the worst cell of all—oneself.

Graham Greene

I had traveled past St. Luke's Hospital in Bellingham hundreds of times, never dreaming I'd be stuck in their emergency room, wheezing for breath.

As I sat waiting in the ER on that summer day so many years ago, it didn't occur to me that I was placing a great deal of trust in these nurses and doctors. I didn't think about whether they knew what they were doing, whether they had been trained in treating asthmatics, or whether they had my best interests in mind.

My situation was urgent, and I needed their help. I trusted them implicitly.

Why did I trust them? Why didn't I waltz into the emergency room and demand to see their credentials? Why didn't I grill them on their choice of medications for me, the results they hoped for, and the possible side effects?

Such challenges would have been preposterous. I trusted them because they worked for a hospital. They'd been trained to help and heal sick people—and I was one sick puppy.

I also knew that doctors and nurses received a great deal of training.

At the time, I didn't know the extent of that training or the specifics of it, but I did know that most people trusted their doctors and complied accordingly.

That's what I chose to do.

In that setting at that time, I welcomed the smell of antiseptic. I relished the fact that the doctors and nurses wore scrubs and booties. I liked the small rooms with curtains around the beds, the medical table, and the drawers overflowing with gauze, tape, sponges, and other supplies. The medical staff was slightly stiff and very professional. Everyone was earnest about his or her role.

From the sterile environment to the formal professionalism, every detail had been carefully prepared, and this preparation screamed "trust." These people knew what they were doing.

Other more routine examples of trust occur daily. For example, consider the act of driving a car. We trust that the engine will start each and every morning as we prepare for work, and we trust that other drivers on the road will stay in their respective lanes, leave sufficient room between themselves and other cars, and move in the proper direction. Were any of these factors to go awry, the results would be catastrophic.

People are counted on daily to avoid mistakes while driving, while building campfires, while constructing bridges, while dispensing medications. People trust me to give them the best counsel possible and to assist them in putting their relational and marital lives back together.

Trust is not simply the glue that holds society together; it's the bedrock of relationships and marriages as well. Trust is the outcome of two aspects of relating we've talked about: stability and safety. When trust dissolves, crisis ensues.

What Is Trust?

Trust is that interdependent relationship between mates, whereby they depend on each other for help in obtaining their goals.

Think about it. When you met your mate, you shared an implicit agreement that you would try to meet one another's needs. You showed an active interest in each other, in your lives, your values, and your goals. You both spoke encouraging words about your interests and objectives, and by doing so, you implied that you would help each other meet those goals.

Without saying as much, you both entered into an agreement. It looked something like this:

We will be available to one another emotionally.

We will encourage one another during good times and bad.

We will create a safe and predictable environment where we can say what we think and feel what we feel.

We will create stability for one another in a place free from any intentional harm.

We will respect boundaries of fidelity and faithfulness.

As the relationship progressed, this agreement became even more implicit, but then on one magical day—your wedding day—the agreement became explicit. You promised to love and to honor your mate. Before saying "I do," you built a huge bridge of trust based on the agreements noted above. With friends and family as witnesses, you pronounced a commitment to maintain that bridge of trust in the future.

The Fragile Bridge

Although our intentions were honorable, many of us entered into this agreement without realizing how much maintenance work was needed to fulfill our promise.

Oh sure, we said we'd love and cherish. With stars in our eyes, we committed to loving our mate until our dying days. But we didn't take time to look into the future. We naively promised love but had our fingers crossed behind our backs in regards to trust. It is almost as if we said, "I'll love you as long as things are easy and enjoyable. But I'm not sure about maintaining the trust. That might take too much work."

Trust is absolutely necessary for any healthy relationship, and we must understand that trust is fragile—it can be broken very easily. If we don't keep that in focus, knowing we can violate trust in a moment, if we don't recognize it may take days, months, or even years to rebuild, we will be in serious trouble. We can damage this fragile bond in countless ways.

Stinging words are spoken during an argument: a violation of trust.

One of you walks out the door, leaving the other panicking over abandonment issues: a violation of trust.

A demeaning gesture is made, suggesting your mate's words were ridiculous: a violation of trust.

You confided in someone of the opposite sex when you were hurt by your mate's behavior: a violation of trust.

You encouraged someone to side with you during an argument: a violation of trust.

You see how it goes. Although we still love our mate, marriage crises bring an onslaught of troubling feelings. We're not sure how to express our anger, so we repeat old behavior patterns and destroy that fragile bridge of trust. We inadvertently make mistakes, further eroding the trust. Without it, we're left standing on one side of the Grand Canyon, our mate is on the other, and we're both wondering what happened.

We failed to consider the importance of maintaining the trust. We failed to recognize that we must not hurt our mate simply because we've been hurt. We must not use harsh words simply because someone else used harsh words. As I mentioned in the previous chapter, each time we do these things, we make huge withdrawals from the love bank. More importantly, we undermine the pillars that support our bridge of trust.

When the bridge begins to creak and sway, most of us retreat. We begin to create our own alternate bypass, thereby intensifying the marriage crisis. Safety and stability erode along with trust.

Foundations of Trust

Many of us take trust for granted. We often believe others will do what they say they're going to do without considering the wisdom of that assumption. Realizing that emotional fidelity is something that can be built and broken, more and more people are critically analyzing the trustworthiness of friends, business partners, and potential mates. A little broken trust goes a long way to increase fear and distrust in the future. We're taking time to consider whether a person is really willing to play by the rules, abide by their agreements, and act in an honorable manner.

In doing so, we evaluate whether people are *capable* of being trusted. When we deem others as trustworthy, we allow them into our lives. If some people are not trustworthy, we do well to keep them at a distance.

When evaluating people's trustworthiness, we also evaluate their *integrity*. Are they people of character? Do they have enough moral fiber to understand the importance of the bridge of trust and their part in maintaining it? Or do they violate trust on whim?

Consider the couple I referred to in the last chapter—Zane and Marsha. Marsha initially deemed Zane capable of providing for many of her emotional and relational needs. This was a questionable judgment call on her part, given what she has discovered about him. She initially determined he had the integrity to do what he said he would do. Although he said he loved her and wanted to marry her, he then emotionally distanced himself by watching television nonstop, failing to keep himself fit and attractive, and bringing work home at night. Marsha began to have questions about his trustworthiness as well as his integrity.

Finally, every bridge of trust is also built upon people's *goodwill* to reach out to their mate and actively meet their needs. This can be challenging when painful emotions are running high and people are angry, discouraged, and busy nursing their wounds.

Marsha is disillusioned. She expected her mate to be available every evening to listen to her talk about her day, to comfort her in her distress, to participate in her daily life. She has reason to be extremely discouraged because Zane lives in and enjoys his work world and only occasionally attaches himself emotionally to Marsha. She feels abandoned and frightened. Would this marriage dissolve like her previous one, leaving her alone and ashamed?

Yet she must consider her part in this mess—a tendency to nag, to be inconsistent in voicing her concerns, and to develop a hostile and critical spirit. She must strive to maintain goodwill toward Zane while not enabling his immature behavior. Listen to the words of the apostle Paul on this subject:

> If you have any encouragement from being united with Christ, if any comfort from his love, if any fellowship with the Spirit, if any tenderness and compassion, then make my joy complete by being like-minded, having the same love, being one in spirit and purpose. Do nothing out of selfish ambition or vain conceit, but in humility consider others better than yourselves. Each of you should look not only to your own interests, but also to the interests of others (Philippians 2:1-4).

Zane and Marsha have a responsibility to consider each other's needs as well as their own. They must exercise goodwill, even in times of crisis—especially in times of crisis! Yet they must manage these volatile emotions, maintaining open and honest communication, honoring decisions they've made, and steering clear of violations of trust.

Ability, integrity, and goodwill are the three pillars that sustain our bridge of trust. When any of these is damaged or absent, our bridge collapses, leaving us looking at our mate across a great chasm that can be spanned only with a great deal of work.

If you find yourself in this predicament, consider your own trustworthiness. How have you done when it comes to keeping agreements, being predictable, and meeting your mate's needs?

Partnership Is a Choice

None of us wants to think about mutual responsibility. We lean away from our obligations in making marriage work or in resolving crises. But marriage is a partnership, a team-building experience.

We've entered into this partnership by choice. We decided to link up with our mate, for better or worse, and we are responsible to maintain the fragile bridge of trust regardless of what our mate might do to us.

Cherie Carter-Scott, in her book *If Love Is a Game, These Are the Rules,* says this about partnership:

> Before you proceed down the road of choosing a partner or not, it helps first to understand exactly what a true partnership is. A partnership is a union between two entities. Partnerships of any kind are formed when both people believe that a greater benefit lies in uniting energies, talents and resources than in remaining separate.[1]

Scott goes on to say what has been aptly described in Scripture as two becoming one flesh, or as Scott says, the "I" becomes "We." While neither "I" is obliterated, "both are enhanced by the chemical fusion with the other. Becoming a 'we' reality means that you form a team whose intent is to travel through life together as a united force."

Notice her words—"we...together as a united force." But crises have a way of pitting one mate against another, and suddenly the team is divided. The Scriptures predict that "every city or household divided against itself will not stand." How true!

Take a moment to consider something very important. Do you still want to be married? Yes, he's a chump at times. Sure, she's self-centered and demanding on occasion. Still, do you want to be married? Do you really want to partner with this person along the path of life? If so, let's broaden our knowledge about the importance and extremely fragile nature of trust.

A Broken Bridge

As you read this book, you may find yourself disillusioned and painfully alone. You may wonder how you've gotten here and how to rebuild the bridge with your mate.

You long for reconciliation. You yearn for those lovely, carefree days when your relationship was young and vibrant, when you could trust your mate with your life. But you also realize that things must change if trust is to be reestablished.

As we move through this book, our number one concern is restoring the trust and vibrancy you once knew. Before exploring avenues for rebuilding this vital causeway, we must explore the reasons trust has been lost. You may notice overlap between some of these violations and those situations that destroy safety and stability. Safety, stability, and trust are all pillars supporting your marriage. If any are missing, you'll find yourself in trouble.

Abandonment

Marsha felt abandoned by Zane. He wasn't gone for weeks at a time, nor did he appear to be unfaithful. He was, however, in love with his work. Additionally, he seemed insensitive to Marsha's emotional and spiritual needs. This abandonment has been devastating for Marsha. Desperately wanting companionship with her husband, she has pleaded with him to participate emotionally in their marriage, but Zane seems lost in another world. Does he ever notice his marriage is on the line and he's in danger of losing his wife?

Abandonment is obviously very destructive. We were made for relationship, and when mates walk away, they leave a gaping hole. When we aren't sure that our mate will be available emotionally, we feel threatened and insecure.

Betrayal

One of the most profound violations of trust is emotional and sexual infidelity. Over the years, both men and women have poured out their hearts to me, agonizing over a mate's betrayal. Whether it happens once or twenty times, the damage is horrific.

Most extramarital affairs begin not as sexual encounters, but as the aftermath of emotional abandonment. Men and women, plagued by chronic loneliness, seek companionship from a ready listener. What begins innocently often ends in a heart-rending affair, and once this occurs, picking up the pieces is challenging at best. Once a heart has been shattered and trust violated to its deepest core, words are rarely enough to heal the wounds. Professional help and years of recovery are needed.

Unfaithfulness

Unfaithfulness can take many different forms. Although we immediately think of sexual infidelity, many couples struggle intensely over unfaithfulness involving family finances, gambling problems, or issues with rage and anger. Couples in blended families quarrel over loyalty issues. These too are violations of trust and betrayals of another kind.

Violations of trust can occur in nearly any arena of marriage, and recovering from these violations can be difficult. Anytime there is deception or evasion of truth, trust disintegrates.

Loyalty

Loyalty is a key component in any healthy relationship. William Bennett, in *The Book of Virtues,* expounds on the importance of loyalty:

> Loyalty is like courage in that it shows itself most clearly when we are operating under stress. Real loyalty endures inconvenience, withstands temptation, and does not cringe under assault. Yet the trust that loyalty tends to generate can pervade our whole lives.[2]

Bennett hits the mark: Loyalty generates trust. When the chips are down and you're struggling to find a way back to your mate, consider loyalty. Consider sticking it out during these difficult times, not because the path is easy and the way is clear, but because it's the right thing to do.

Loyalty says, "I will extend my hand to you again, cautiously, carefully, with some hesitation. I will do my part to rebuild the bridge of trust because I want to be there for you, and I want you to be there for me. Neither of us has been fully trustworthy. But together we can build a new bond and begin to care for one another again."

You can see that rebuilding trust requires courage. It means setting aside the painful feelings of the past and deliberately moving forward in the relationship.

"But I can't forget what he's done to me," you say. "If I trust him, he'll just hurt me again."

You'll have to step back and decide if this relationship is worth saving. If it is, you'll need to find a way to move forward.

Creating Room for Trust

Trust doesn't develop in a vacuum. Like a precious flower, your marriage needs nutrients. You cannot provide those nutrients if you're bristling with hostility and distrust.

The 12 steps of Alcoholics Anonymous promotes a useful technique: "Fake it until you make it." What this means is that even though you *feel* distrust, you practice creating a space for trust to be rebuilt. You act in trustworthy ways. You're purposeful about promoting behaviors that instill confidence, such as abiding by agreements and remaining emotionally and sexually faithful.

We have already briefly considered another powerful strategy: conflict containment.

Conflict containment is the art of setting aside differences until you're in a safe place, such as counseling, where you can explore heated issues. You haven't found a way to tackle these issues alone in a productive manner, so place them in a leak-proof container, high on a shelf, to be taken down only when you've demonstrated that you can do so without injuring each other.

Through the use of time-outs and conflict containment, you can create a space for trust and love to grow once again. But while containing conflict is essential, it is not enough. You must also plant some seeds and pull some weeds.

Eliminating the weeds from your troubled relationship means tackling and resolving issues. You simultaneously plant seeds of goodness in your relationship. You "fake it until you make it," showing kindness and tenderness even when doing so may feel like a stretch. Pulling weeds and planting seeds creates space for love and trust to blossom again.

Strategies for Restoring Trust

If you've been violated in some egregious way, or if the trust violations have occurred repeatedly, rebuilding the bond becomes even more challenging. The following strategies can be very helpful in moving past anger and pettiness so that you can restore the trust to your relationship.

- Attend to the trust violations. Agree on goals for rebuilding trust. Wherever a breach has occurred, make agreements that will reduce the chance that it will happen again.
- Agree to learn how and why the violations occurred and to determine what you each need to do so they don't happen again. Understand and explore any "slippery places" with a strong determination to avoid them.
- Make appropriate amends. The perpetrator needs to show his or her intentions by doing something that shouts "I'm sorry" to the other. In the case of a minor violation, a small token of affection may be enough to restore love and grace to the relationship. To heal after significant unfaithfulness, setting healthier boundaries is a first step. Agreeing to participate in couples' counseling is also a great strategy.
- Generate a list of trust-restoring activities. Along with making amends, a couple must agree on strategies for rebuilding trust, such as keeping agreements. Do what you say you're going to do!
- Quickly apologize when you blow it. Apologies acknowledge wrongdoing and indicate remorse and reassurance for the future. An immediate, heartfelt apology means a

lot because it acknowledges the impact the violation has had on your mate, and it doesn't allow time to establish bitterness.

- Notice gains. Catch one another doing the right things. Comment on these acts of kindness. Enjoy them. Build upon them.
- Communicate accurately, openly, and transparently. No more deception. No more hiding or avoiding issues. Instead of finding fault, seek solutions. Instead of blaming, own your pain. Communicate to your mate what you expect. Communicate empathy to your mate, whether you've been violated or you've been the violator. You both need love.
- Keep expectations manageable. Our goal is to take things one step at a time, building one success upon another. Perhaps you'll agree to meet for a dinner date one night a week.
- Practice trusting. Trust often needs to be given in order for it to be returned. Although you may not feel comfortable completely trusting your mate, you can surely find small ways to extend yourself to each other.

Trusting Yourself

As strange as it sounds, one of the biggest hurdles in rebuilding trust is learning to trust yourself. Ultimately, your mate will let you down in some way at one time or another. He or she may not be available in critical moments of need. You married someone who is fallible and human, just like you. Forgive your partner and yourself, again and again. Develop the capacity to self-soothe, especially when things are tense and you cannot get the nurturance you want. David Schnarch mentions this in his book *Passionate Marriage:*

> It's not safe to love your partner more than you can self-soothe, especially if you always need him or her to "be there

> for you."...Loving is not for the weak, nor for those who have to be carefully kept, nor for the faint of heart.[3]

Self-soothing seems to be a lost art. We don't hear enough about developing the capacity to spend quiet time in prayer, go for long walks, journaling, or getting that occasional massage. Sometimes calling a friend on the phone during a challenging time is enough encouragement to hang in there with a troubling situation.

Even a beloved, wonderful mate will disappoint you at times—just as you will disappoint that person. Deal with it. Get used to the idea that pain enters every life. But through it all you will have learned to trust yourself and God.

Joseph

The Bible contains many accounts of trust—broken, restored, and maintained. Joseph is an example of a man whose family violently betrayed his trust, and yet he didn't allow that betrayal to damage him.

As an overconfident young man, Joseph was the favorite son of Jacob. Because he firmly believed that God had a special design on his life, Joseph was unbearable to his brothers, who conspired to kill him. The brothers devised an intricate murder scheme, but in the end, Joseph was sold to Potiphar, an official to Pharaoh.

Through the ordeal, Joseph trusted God to protect him.

> The LORD was with Joseph and he prospered, and he lived in the house of his Egyptian master. When his master saw that the LORD was with him and that the LORD gave him success in everything he did, Joseph found favor in his eyes and became his attendant. Potiphar put him in charge of his household, and he entrusted to his care everything he owned (Genesis 39:2-5).

You'd think this was enough drama for any man, but his trust in the Lord was about to be tested again.

Joseph was "well-built and handsome," and Potiphar's wife tried to seduce him. Jilted by Joseph's resistance, she accused him of accosting her, and he was thrown in jail. Here again, Joseph shows his integrity and trust in the Lord, and the Lord comes to his aid. In time Joseph is given another opportunity to gain favor with Pharaoh by interpreting his dreams. Eventually, Joseph is placed in charge of all of Egypt.

In a most poignant ending to this story of incredible trust and obedience, Joseph meets his brothers, who had come to Egypt for grain during a famine. Most of us would seize this opportunity for revenge, but not Joseph. He saw the bigger picture—which is a lesson for all of us. Listen to his words.

> Do not be distressed and do not be angry with yourselves for selling me here, because it was to save lives that God sent me ahead of you...So then, it was not you who sent me here, but God...You intended to harm me, but God intended it for good to accomplish what is now being done, the saving of many lives (Genesis 45:5,8; 50:20).

The lesson is clear: Even during a marital crisis, you must trust God to work in your life. Although you cannot see the outcome to your current struggle, you must seize every opportunity to become the person God desires you to be. You must consider the bigger picture, trusting God when you cannot fully trust your mate, or perhaps even yourself. God loves you and desires the best for you.

> Trust in the Lord with all your heart and do not lean on your own understanding; in all your ways acknowledge him, and he will make your paths straight (Proverbs 3:5-6).

5

Determining the Causes of Your Crisis

I am walking over hot coals suspended over a deep pit at the bottom of which are a large number of vipers baring their fangs.

John Major

A crisis is something we're not prepared to handle that creates tremendous anxiety in our lives.

I vividly remember one spring morning, seven years ago, when my close friend Randy called me, telling me he'd packed up his car, preparing for an extended stay at his vacation home. His wife had announced that she wanted time alone to think about the direction of her life.

Hardly able to breathe, and certainly unable to think straight, Randy asked me to meet him for lunch in town, several miles away. I immediately left my office and headed for the restaurant.

We met in the restaurant parking lot. Like a confident medic, I placed my hand on his shoulder and created a space for him to vent. I invited him to share his story, knowing he needed to talk things out. Fighting back tears, Randy shared that weeks earlier, his wife hinted at the separation. He said he did his best to change her mind, but to no avail. After pausing for a moment, he simply cried.

Anatomy of a Crisis

Crises are daunting because they tax your resources beyond your ability to cope. If your situation were a routine struggle, we'd call it that. You'd know how to handle it, and you wouldn't need to read this book (unless you're helping others).

But this is not a routine struggle. It's not a minor disagreement that you can resolve quickly. It's a crisis, and you're uncertain as to how to navigate these perilous waters. No one leaves a marriage emergency unscathed.

Let's look more closely at what happens in a typical crisis. To prepare you to make decisions about your relationship, let's consider where you and your mate are in this cycle.[1]

Stage One: Mounting Tension

During this stage, the couple realizes they have problems, but they try to maintain a steady state, often by employing resistance and denial. They feel the water rising, intuitively sensing they're losing ground but not wanting to admit they're in a crisis. One or both partners are likely to say, "I know we've got problems, but I think we can handle them."

As things progress, both people use more and more denial to maintain equilibrium. Because tension is mounting, they know at some level that what they're doing is not bringing the problem under control. Still, old behavior patterns die hard, and they may keep doing the same things, hoping for different results. This never works.

Stage Two: Plateau of Disorganization

Eventually, one or both mates feel increasingly anxious and begin to realize that established patterns of interacting are doing nothing to fix the problems. Anxiety increases. Both partners may become frantic as they come to grips with the realization that their marriage is spinning out of control.

Denial may increase during this phase, even with the realization that it isn't working and that it's taking more and more effort to keep the problems under control.

Stage Three: Mobilization of Internal and External Resources

Finally, one or both mates begin to frantically explore ways to settle the crisis. In an effort to find answers, they may seek counsel from anyone and everyone.

During this phase of Randy's marital crisis, he was desperate for answers, desperate for advice from anyone who could fix his problems. Unfortunately, being open to all forms of counsel also created confusion because he received both good and bad advice and often struggled to discern the difference.

Randy shared one particular piece of bad counsel from his former pastor during the initial stages of his marriage crisis. Even though his wife had asked for a separation, his pastor told him not to leave their home under any circumstances. "Make her leave if she wants a separation," he said. "Make it hard on her since she's the one who wants the space."

This seemed like wise advice at the time because it put the onus for the separation on her. He now believes this counsel was unnecessarily punitive and harsh and served only to anger his wife. She was angry at the pastor for "forcing her out" instead of honoring her wish for him to leave. She felt pushed away from caring church members.

In the midst of a crisis, any raft looks inviting, but in fact many have more holes than the ship you're on. Be careful. This is a time to weigh out counsel, pray, and take the course of action that seems the wisest.

Stage Four: Adaptation and Maladaptation

Although your immediate crisis may not be resolved in the manner you wish, it will be resolved. As they say, "This too shall pass."

Crises are usually resolved in one of three ways: (a) adaptation of mind-set, which involves dealing with the crisis in a positive way;

(b) adaptation to new circumstances, such as coming to terms with a separation, divorce, or another life change; or (c) maladaptation—settling back into old, dysfunctional ways of interacting. Every crisis offers an opportunity for change.

In a recent counseling session, a middle-aged woman, Laura, and her husband, Darrin, discussed his anger. Specifically, they came to counseling after a particularly troubling outburst in which Darrin screamed at Laura because she had left his shop door open and the light on. Laura left their home temporarily, agreeing to return under the condition that they seek counseling.

A 55-year-old professional, Laura is quite assertive. Somehow, however, she had settled into allowing Darrin to have temper tantrums periodically, with only an occasional scolding as a response. After this most recent episode, however, she moved from stage one (mounting tension) and stage two (disorganization) to stage three (mobilization of resources). Laura called a friend for support, and the friend recommended my services.

Darrin was a bit aloof during our initial session. Slowly, however, after seeing that Laura was not going to tolerate such outbursts in the future, he warmed to me and the counseling process.

"Laura says you've got a pattern of blowing up over seemingly trivial matters," I said.

"She's right. But she's gotten my attention now. I guess it's time to work on it."

Laura and Darrin agreed to continue counseling to explore his patterns of anger as well as her patterns of enabling him to have his outbursts without significant consequences. He understood that if he did not work on his problem, she would move out. They advanced fairly quickly into a new, adaptive pattern of functioning and were able to resolve their crisis.

Other couples are less fortunate. Not catching their crisis in time, they move into adapting to new circumstances, such as a marital separation or divorce. Still others settle back into old ways of relating, either ignoring the cancer that threatens their marriage or leaving the marriage and taking all their well-established, dysfunctional ways of interacting with them. Some jump from one crisis to another a short time later. Changing partners is not the way to learn the skills necessary to build a healthy relationship.

Causes of Crises

Scott Peck introduced his famous book *The Road Less Traveled* with this line: "Life is difficult." He could just as easily have said, "Marriage is difficult," or "Relationships are next to impossible. Enter at your own risk."

Anyone who has been engaged in a relationship or marriage for more than a few months knows the truth of these words. Marriage and relating are difficult work and can easily lead to crisis. If we don't manage problems effectively, they have the power to erode the foundation of the marriage. They can cause alienation, distrust, and isolation, ultimately leading to a collapse of the marriage.

And why shouldn't marriage be hard? So often, we are unprepared for it. Consider this scene:

A 25-year-old man from Seattle attends the University of Washington. He has hoped for many years to be accepted by the university and plans to go on to medical school like his father and grandfather. He has been raised in a liberal church, attending infrequently. He is outgoing, somewhat aggressive, and definitely goal-oriented.

He meets a pretty young woman, a bit shy and overprotected, whom he enjoys and is attracted to. She too has always dreamed of attending the university but comes from a very different background. Raised in a very conservative, devout Christian home, she is considering attending seminary after graduation. Her long-term goal is doing mission work or working with inner-city youth.

She appreciates his daring attitude and his ambitious pursuit of her. He appreciates her softness and willingness to allow him to protect her.

This is all well and good, but does this relationship have enough commonalities to survive? Neither person has learned an ounce of skill in Relationships 101. They don't know how to communicate effectively about difficult topics, have never read a word about conflict management, and don't know about negotiation or sharing. How can they possibly survive the rigors of relating, let alone marriage?

This scene happens, of course, hundreds of times each day. Infatuation and attraction form the basis of "hooking up," and then the couple struggles to create an enduring relationship. Many times they cannot.

However, all is not lost. Although problems are part of marriage, we don't have to succumb to them. In order to handle crises more effectively, we must understand what causes them and learn what we can do to prevent or solve them.

Why do so many marriages falter, and what can we learn about these problems so that we can grow from them? Taking on too narrow a focus is tempting. For example, we might blame sexual differences, money struggles, or fights about in-laws for creating the marriage crisis. Such blaming would be incorrect.

The problem is the process!

Although we might technically be correct to say the crisis stemmed from an unstable condition in the marriage, we would be more accurate to say that the couple didn't have the internal resources to navigate that unstable condition and resolve the crisis.

If a wife, for example, repeatedly spends too much money, leaving the husband bitter and angry, should we say that money is the problem?

No.

The way she spent money certainly irritated him. But the *process* is the problem. The couple doesn't have the skills to talk about her need to spend money, about her violations of their marital boundaries, if they have any, or about how to avoid escalating the conflict.

Most crises are the result of some external issue—not enough sex, too much spending, bitterness about in-laws, differences in parenting strategies—and these differences, if unresolved, lead to disastrous long-term effects on the marriage.

Every couple, especially those in crisis, must find a place where they can not only talk about sex, money, in-laws, and the like, but also explore *the way they talk* about these issues. Now we're back to what we discussed in earlier chapters:

the importance of creating safety in the marriage

the importance of creating security in the marriage

the importance of creating trust in the marriage

And of course we can't forget the importance of creating a process whereby we can talk about anything, in a *safe, controlled, and effective environment.* The way out of a crisis will be through a refined, healthy pattern of interacting.

Causes Beneath the Crisis

A crisis doesn't simply occur out of the blue. Both partners have most likely already tried to manage the crisis—often through the use of denial. They wished, hoped, prayed, and pretended that things would be okay, only to find their relationship was in serious trouble.

She may tolerate his drinking for years until he "forgets" to come home one evening. He may tolerate her controlling nature until she lashes out at him one too many times in front of their friends. She tires of his distancing maneuvers and finally withdraws herself to the point of wondering if she'll ever connect with him again. Another woman offers him an alternative to her nagging, and he falls victim to a night of meaningless sex.

Many of us ignore problems until they grow so large we can ignore them no longer. Many times these problems are insidious. Invariably, when I sit with a couple dissecting their marriage, they're able to see the signs and symptoms in their rearview mirror. Jesus said, "Every good tree bears good fruit, but a bad tree bears bad fruit" (Matthew 7:17). Weeds grow from soil that has not been cultivated; good fruit grows on plants that have been nourished and tended.

The same is true of marriage. Looking deep within the troubled relationship, we find the problems: dishonesty, discord, and other negative behavior patterns. The partners may not have seen the crisis coming, but when we explore their history, they see fractures that developed years ago. They see how both became less vulnerable and less intimate with one another; they became involved in outside activities to the point of ignoring the need for time together; they gave up attending church and maintaining a rich spiritual life. The signs and symptoms were there all along.

Small Things Become Big

Many marriages in crisis have several aspects in common.

Loss of Love and Intimacy

The loss of love and intimacy can be both a cause and a result of marital problems. Many people seem to think, perhaps unconsciously, that a marriage will tend itself. One day, however, we walk by the garden and notice it is overgrown with weeds. Shocked to see the garden in such disrepair, we remember that we made the decision to let it take care of itself.

Stephanie Dowrick's book *Forgiveness and Other Acts of Love* includes a particular moving essay on fidelity. In it she makes this comment about faithfulness:

> People can be—and often are—"virtuously" sexually monogamous, while being untrue to the vows of love. Can we call those people "faithful," therefore, when they are angry and abusive to their partner, belittling or sarcastic, or withholding words, affection, money or safety? If so, then we would need to ask, faithful to what and to whom?[2]

A husband and wife may pride themselves on staying together for 43 years, but what if they haven't been intimate in the last 20 and haven't shared their love and affection during that time? Can they really say they've been faithful to one another? The structure and outward trappings of their marriage appear to be alive, but their relational soul is dead. This is the soil from which a crisis sprouts.

Bitterness and Rancor

A couple in crisis often harbors anger. Both partners are wounded, afraid, and perhaps desperate to get even, so the marriage looks more like a battle zone than a love nest. In a marriage filled with bitterness, trust is lost. Each person pulls away, afraid of getting hurt. Like a mollusk that builds layer upon layer of protection, mates insulate themselves from each other.

Recently, I worked with a couple hoping to move toward marriage. Two years earlier Gary and Eva had stars in their eyes and imagined a long life together.

Eva is an attractive, dark-haired woman with a soft and gentle attitude. She has been through two previous marriages in a short time and comes to this relationship wary. Having been hurt by two neglectful and demanding husbands, she was initially encouraged by Gary's kind demeanor.

Gary is handsome and gray-haired, sturdy and muscular. He is more outgoing than Eva and also more forceful. They came to see me for an emergency appointment following an explosion by Eva.

"I'm not usually like that," Eva said, referring to a recent outburst. "I usually withdraw, but I'm sick of withdrawing when Gary tells me what to think and do."

"She's filled with bitterness," Gary said. "She won't even try to get beyond it. She harbors resentment instead of love and kindness."

"It's true," Eva said, appearing ashamed.

"What are you feeling, Eva?" I asked.

"He's right. I'm filled with resentment and bitterness. I take it and take it and finally explode, and then I'm ugly. I've stopped dating Gary several times over the past two months because I don't think he listens to me."

Gary looked on dispassionately as Eva cried.

"What do you think about what she's saying, Gary?"

"I think I've made mistakes," Gary said. "But we've got to let go of resentment and move forward with love."

"It sounds like Eva can't get to the love part because of so much hurt and resentment. It sounds like she needs to feel like you are listening to her and understanding what she has to say before she can stop feeling resentful. Is that possible?"

Gary reluctantly gave some ground, admitting that bitterness had indeed spoiled their relationship. He also acknowledged that this underlying resentment needed attention before Eva could create space for love.

I'm still working with Eva and Gary, helping them heal wounds and behaviors that led to their problems. Only as they succeed in these efforts will they resolve their crisis and move into the love they both want so desperately.

Inability to Solve Problems

Watching Gary and Eva discuss their problems was like walking through a carnival at peak hour—pointed words, sarcasm, pouting, and passive-aggressive behaviors all created chaos and crisis. Eva intermittently reached out to Gary and then recoiled into her chair. She began talking and then abruptly withdrew into near silence. Gary, all the while, remained strangely calm.

As I listened to them present their issues, I was reminded again of the universal truth: The process is the problem. This process problem—distrust, bitterness, and attacking—had led to an inability to solve problems. As problems mounted, barriers to intimacy increased, leading to a crisis. Both Gary and Eva knew they were in trouble. Their cherished relationship, which they had both hoped was leading to marriage, was in big trouble. They hadn't succeeded in building an arena where they could solve problems, and subsequently both faced one another over a mound of resentment.

Betrayal

Perhaps nothing strikes fear in the heart of a married man or woman like betrayal. Sexual betrayal, of course, is the pinnacle of unfaithfulness. Having placed your heart and life in the hands of your mate, imagining your mate in the arms of another lover is more than you can process. All systems shut down under an onslaught of questions that never leave the mind.

"How could you do this to me?"

"What have I ever done to you to cause you to do this?"

"How did you meet him?"

"Why her?"

"How do I know this won't happen again?"

And the questions go on and on, over and over again. The problem is too big, too momentous, too much to process. That's why it's a crisis.

In the ensuing weeks, months, and years, the couple will need to find ways to recover. They must dig deep to create a circle large enough to encompass this tragedy if they are to survive. They must then find that place where they are still longing for acceptance, commitment, intimacy, and love.

Self-Centeredness and Irresponsibility

"I wish you'd grow up." Couples in crisis often talk that way. So many crises could be avoided if we gave up selfish ambitions, self-centered strivings, and immature power struggles.

Without exception, the rare skirmishes I've had with my wife, Christie, stem from self-centeredness and immaturity. Feeling wounded, we attack. Feeling frightened, we run like children. Having egos bruised, we hurl insults like playground bullies. However, feeling embarrassed and desiring intimacy more than distance, we usually catch ourselves in mid-blow and self-correct. We remind ourselves of biblical principles and allow these truths to change us. But only as we submit to these truths and the power of the Spirit are we transformed. How about you? When threatened, do you take the high road? When hurt, can you share your pain rather than retaliate? Are you striving, as the apostle Peter said, to "grow in the grace and knowledge of our Lord and Savior Jesus Christ" (2 Peter 3:18)?

The Truth Will Set You Free

Your task in this book is to identify the crisis, manage and stabilize it, end it, and move earnestly into restoring your marriage. We've covered some of the most prominent causes of marital crisis, though certainly not all.

Understanding any challenging issue requires several processes. One is *a dedication to the truth.* Although you may resist admitting the reasons he had the affair, you must explore all possibilities so you can rid yourself of the marital cancer. If you collude with your mate to gloss over the relational troubles that led to the crisis and settle instead for the quick fix, you're likely to find yourselves in the same situation down the road. This is not a time for codependent pretending that amounts to little more than hoping the problem will disappear. It's time for strong, brave words of truth.

Another prerequisite on your path to the healing truth is *a spirit of detachment.* You must step back and take a larger view of the landscape. The pursuit of truth must be greater than the desire to protect old, established ways of interacting, as strong as they may be.

The pursuit of healing truth—understanding the causes of crisis—also means *respecting resistance.* Just as surely as you want to understand and overcome the urgency of the moment, you're also committed to not changing a thing. Like an old computer, we all have default settings, entrenched ways of operating that are powerful and reinforced daily. Facing the truth means understanding established patterns and being willing to overcome resistance to change.

Jesus knew seeking the truth would be difficult when He said, "If you hold to my teaching, you are really my disciples. Then you will know the truth, and the truth will set you free" (John 8:31-32).

God's truth offers us hope and healing. It provides direction for our lives. Moreover, when we hide it in our heart, it transforms and heals us.

Our task is to know God's truths and hold fast to them. The power of God in our lives will cause us to lead lives free from irresponsibility, bitterness, and betrayal. Because of the Spirit's work in our lives, we will want to take the higher road of love rather than the lower road of selfish desires. I encourage you, as you strive for an escape from this emergent situation, to embrace the Spirit of God and invite Him to help you seek truth and ultimate healing.

6

Responding to Your Wake-Up Call

Life is a process of becoming, a combination of states we have to go through. Where people fail is that they wish to elect a state and remain in it. This is a kind of death.

Anaïs Nin

"You have to completely change the way you're doing things if you want to live beyond 40," the doctor said.

"What?" I asked incredulously.

"You're living an unhealthy lifestyle. It's an invitation for more problems with asthma, and I can guarantee we'll see you in the hospital again and again if things don't change."

By the time I had this conversation, I had already been hospitalized three or four times, for several days each time, as doctors tried to manage my asthma.

I didn't want to adjust my lifestyle. I was 22 and thought I was invincible even though I was dabbling with behaviors that aggravated my condition. I enjoyed an occasional cigarette in smoky lounges or bars with college buddies. I had two long-haired Irish setters and a cat. I lived in a dusty apartment with shag carpeting.

These were all taboo for an asthmatic who was taking several medications, including steroids and weekly allergy injections. But I didn't want to quit smoking, give up my pets, or stop hanging out in bars.

Simply put, I didn't want to change.

Finally, in a desperate effort to breathe normally, I decided to consult a specialist in Seattle, a two-hour drive from Bellingham. It had taken weeks to get the appointment.

Dr. J. David Hansen was a tall, gray-haired man, stiff in his presentation. He was a specialist in pulmonary illnesses, and I hoped he might save me from regular hospitalization and a lifetime of medication. I hadn't told my primary care physician about some of my destructive behaviors. By the time I faced Dr. Hansen, I knew it was time to be completely honest. After a curt greeting, he looked up at me from the inventory I had filled out.

"You're an occasional smoker?"

"Yep," I answered glibly. "But not a steady smoker."

"And you have two dogs?"

"They're beautiful Irish setters."

"And a cat?" he asked.

I nodded.

"Look, David," he said, closing my chart. "I'm not sure I want to work with you. I don't know if you're more interested in trying to kill yourself or get better. I don't know if you like smoking more than you like living, or if you like dander and dust more than you like breathing. I'm in the business of helping people heal, not watching them die."

I stared at Dr. Hansen in disbelief as he continued. "I'm not going to help you kill yourself, David. I'm going to tell you some things, and then I want you to think them over before coming back to see me. I'm not going to have you waste my time. Either we work together to save your life and breath, or we shake hands and part ways."

Although I was tired of going to the hospital, until now I figured I could still have it both ways. I thought I could dabble with smoking, go to Reno a few times a year to gamble in smoky casinos, enjoy my pets, and visit the tavern on Saturdays after work with my buddies. But Dr. Hansen gave me a wake-up call.

"Here's the bottom line," he said, peering over his half-glasses and towering above me as I sat on his bench. "Your lungs sound horrible.

They're a sticky, gooey mess. You've got a straight shot at emphysema and an early death if you don't change. You'll have to give up cigarettes completely along with your pets. And no trips to bars or taverns. You must live in places that have wood or linoleum floors—no shag carpets. You'll have to develop a healthy lifestyle. I'm willing to work on a new medication regimen for you but only if you take this situation seriously."

When I started to respond, Dr. Hansen held up his hand to stop me.

"I don't want your answer now," he said. "This is no game. You've probably never sat in a room with someone who was sucking on an oxygen machine for every breath. Even if you had witnessed that, I'm guessing you wouldn't believe it could happen to you. You're young, strong, and determined. But you're going to die an early death if you don't change your behaviors. Think about it. Life or death. Give me a call in two weeks if you want to work with me. If not, I wish you well."

The Cold Truth

Sometimes, during and after a crisis, you sit quietly for a moment with the unvarnished truth. If you're wise, you pay attention and avert further calamity. If you're tuned in at all, you consider what your situation is telling you. That's what Solomon did: "When times are good, be happy; but when times are bad, consider: God has made the one as well as the other" (Ecclesiastes 7:14).

These were bad times for me, and it was time to consider making a change. The specialist told me in no uncertain terms that this was my only hope for better breathing. He said the only way for me to avoid spending my future hooked to an oxygen tank was to give up the behaviors that were harming me. If I wanted Dr. Hansen to treat me—and my primary doctor told me that I did—then I would have to change.

Dr. Hansen, however, wasn't content to simply give me the cold, hard truth. He also offered me a choice: If I wanted him to treat me, I would have to comply with his recommendations. I could no longer have a foot in each camp—simultaneously wanting to change and wanting things to stay exactly the same. Or, more precisely, wanting to get better without having to give up anything.

Dr. Hansen didn't stop there. He made it clear that I was choosing either life or death. He also gave me the responsibility of making the decision myself.

Of course, Dr. Hansen knew what he was doing when he formulated this proposition. Let's see—I could make lifestyle changes that would keep me out of the emergency room and allow me to breathe freely, or I could keep hacking my lungs out, gasping for breath, sniffling and sneezing and scratching and itching. The choice became easier the more I thought about it.

Sometimes the cold, hard truth is exactly what the doctor ordered. It has a way of putting everything in perspective.

Asleep in Your Marriage

I've always disliked alarms, whether they're coming from emergency medical vehicles or clocks. I dislike anything that rattles my nerves or rousts me from sleep.

But alarms are also helpful. We rely on them to wake us, to alert us that it's time to shift gears. Alarms help us change directions, especially when we're heading toward trouble or content to sleep our lives away. In the same way, we need alarms that are particularly jangling during our days of marital crisis. We need something to awaken us from our emotional sleep.

Most of us sleepwalk through life. Sadly, most people will face their crises while still asleep. Even though their adrenaline is pumping and they're scared half out of their minds, they're still emotionally and spiritually asleep!

How is this possible, you wonder? How can we move through life only half awake to where we're going, how we got there, and what we're going to do about it?

The answer is *habituation,* a fancy word I learned in graduate school that says that after a period of time we will stop responding to a certain stimulus. We become numb, anesthetized to a problem. We shut off the alarm.

If you've been with your mate more than three months, you've probably already begun to respond in patterned ways. You react to problems in patterned ways, you communicate in patterned ways, you avoid problems in patterned ways, and you even listen to new information in patterned ways. We habituate to our world, and subsequently we walk around asleep, in desperate need of a wake-up call.

Habituation is perfectly illustrated in the story of the frog in the kettle. In this tale, the frog jumps out of boiling water, but if the water heats up slowly, it remains in the kettle and eventually dies.

I talk with habituated people every day in my office. The conversations prior to the wake-up call often sound something like this:

"Folks, you really need to change some things if you hope to avoid a marriage meltdown," I say.

"We know," they reply. "But we're busy and aren't sure we can create time for counseling sessions. Besides, we've got other bills to pay, and counseling would stretch the budget. We'll check back with you in a few months."

Here's how the conversation typically goes a few months later when they're in a crisis:

"Doc, we need an appointment right away. Our marriage is in trouble. Can you help us?"

What a difference a crisis makes in waking us up to our problems. Listening to our wake-up call means *paying attention*. You notice things you didn't notice in the past. You practice skills you've never practiced before. In some ways, this will be frightening because you're no longer asleep—and sleep can be a very pleasant thing. But you'll be relationally alive rather than settling for a dying marriage.

The Truth About Marriage

Alarms awaken us to the realities of life. As with my medical emergency, your marriage crisis requires facing the truth. You know that it's time to make some decisions. You cannot keep doing what you've always done, or you'll soon be facing marital death. It's not just that you have an opportunity to change—you *must* change. You *must* face the facts, and some of them are very difficult to accept.

Emergencies have a way of slapping us in the face with the truth. Marital emergencies suddenly bring issues into focus.

"We can't ignore our problems any longer," a couple might say. "We've neglected things for a long time, but the truth is, we're in trouble."

Crises are never enjoyable, but in retrospect, these troubling times bring our situation into focus. That is one way the truth sets us free. The truth clarifies our circumstances and forces us to make decisions. Sometimes we make wise choices that bring renewal and joy; sometimes we make poor choices that hurt us. In each case, we're allowed to decide.

Your marriage is in crisis. You didn't wake up yesterday and decide things were out of control. No, in fact you've known things were in a downward spiral for some time. Although you didn't want to face the facts, you're not surprised when they emerge and you find yourself in a troubling situation.

Scott Peck informs us that one of the most critical issues in this process of rebuilding a marriage pertains to our dedication to the truth. The wake-up call is the alert, and responding honestly to the call is vital.

> The more clearly we see the reality of the world, the better equipped we are to deal with the world. The less clearly we see the reality of the world—the more our minds are befuddled by falsehood, misperceptions and illusions—the less able we will be to determine correct courses of action and make wise decisions.[1]

The choice is clear—to remain deluded, hiding in a world we've constructed to keep us safe and warm, or to face the world the way it really is so we can make healthy decisions about our marriage.

The facts are staring you in the face. It's decision time, time to determine how badly you want a different life and marriage.

A Commitment to Change

"Take some time to think it over," Dr. Hansen advised. In fact, he insisted that I take time to consider my options. He knew something that many of us take a long time to understand: A decision made glibly and impetuously is no decision at all. That's an *impulse,* and it rarely sustains itself in any positive way.

In my 31 years of counseling, I've found that most couples drop out of the counseling process rather than stick it out to a point where they've reached complete healing. This should come as no surprise. We're a nation of quick fixes, bailing wire and chewing gum repairs, and cosmetic solutions. Rarely are we ready and willing to face the truth of our problems and commit to life-changing transformation, especially if it requires real, long-term sacrifice and attention.

My favorite example of what commitment to change entails is about a couple who came to see me because of the husband's gambling addiction. Both in their fifties, they could have come straight out of a high-gloss fashion magazine. He wore neatly pressed khakis and a Tommy Bahama shirt. She was decked out in the latest fashions as well, with a sleek black skirt, a contrasting blouse, and tall heels. Both were slim and fit, every hair perfectly in place. If you judged solely by appearance, Joe and Carley seemed on the top of the world.

I asked why they had come to see me.

"He's got a gambling addiction," she said, "and I never know if he's going to spend our paycheck on the cards."

The mood in the room quickly changed from overt friendliness to avoidance and defensiveness.

"It's not that bad," Joe said. "When's the last time I blew a bunch of money? I've really been watching it."

"I'll admit that he's been better lately," Carley said, "but I never know when it's going to happen again. I can't count on our money lasting from month to month."

Over the next 30 minutes, I explored Joe's history with gambling. Some nights he'd stayed out until two or three in the morning without even bothering to call. Feeling guilty and caught up in his addiction, he turned off his phone, which only added to Carley's anxiety.

Joe had a serious problem. He demonstrated all the traits of someone hoping to recoup lost money by hitting a single jackpot. He felt the shame and remorse of those caught in the grips of addiction, but still he refused to face the severity of his problem.

Carley's mood plummeted as we talked about the many evenings of uncertainty, wondering if Joe would come home, if he'd spent their grocery money, and if he'd admit that he needed treatment. After weeks of doing better, a recent episode where he gambled away their paychecks prompted her to call my office in a moment of panic.

"I called because I can't live like this anymore," Carley said. "My life's completely unpredictable because he brings chaos into our lives. I love him, but things have to change."

"Honey," Joe said softly, reaching for her hand. "Things are changing. I'm getting on top of this. You don't need to worry. You've got to admit, my lapses have been fewer and fewer over the last year. And besides, I won money the last time out."

Joe's denial was typical. He was saying all the things addicts say. He minimized, rationalized, denied, and made excuses for his gambling.

As we neared the end of the session, I explained that I thought their marriage was in critical condition. I told them that Joe's gambling was a cancer in their relationship, that radical surgery would be necessary to remove the cancer but that it could be done. However, both of them would have to make a commitment to change.

Just as I was getting ready to schedule their next appointment, Carley turned to me.

"Actually, I think we're going to be okay," she said. "Joe understands the problem and is facing the truth of the matter. I think he's committed to change. I trust him, and we'll call if we need further assistance. You've been very helpful, and we appreciate what you've done for us."

Despite my insistence that they needed professional help, they both emphatically asserted their desire to go it alone. They voiced a hollow commitment to change, but they would do so on their own terms—which in all likelihood meant no change at all.

Carley and Joe didn't answer their wake-up call. They had not reached their bottom. Here they were, sitting with a psychologist who was willing and able to help them deal with Joe's gambling addiction and Carley's codependency, and yet their response was to stand up and walk out of the room.

This story is not unusual. We all would prefer to change without pain. We want to be healed without surgery. We want the hurt to go away without having to confront the root of the problem. Commitment to change is very hard to come by, so the emergency returns again and again.

Honest, Open, and Willing

Every emergency is a wake-up call and an opportunity to answer three fundamental questions. I ask these three of every couple that comes to me in a crisis, knowing their predicament presents an opportunity for change.

1. Are you ready to be honest with yourself about the problem? And I mean completely honest with what brought you to this place. What are the factors that have led to this crisis? How have you contributed, and how do you continue to contribute to the crisis? It's not all about him; it's not all about her. What's your part, and are you willing to examine it? Knowing that a crisis rarely erupts out of thin air, this is a wake-up call to face facts head-on.

2. Are you willing to be open to the change process? This means agreeing to be transparent. You cannot hide behind excuses, rationalizations, and old ways of doing things. You must courageously face your problems, allowing your therapist or pastor to speak into your

life. If you are content doing things the same old way or insist on defending your entrenched behaviors, you're not open.

3. Are you willing to see things from a fresh perspective? As the Alcoholic's Anonymous program asserts, "Your best thinking got you here." That means you must be willing to listen to new counsel. You must loosen your grip on the way you've been viewing your problems. It hasn't been working. You're in trouble. Are you really willing to listen to and heed new counsel?

An honest, open, and willing attitude is very powerful. When a couple comes to one of my marriage intensives ready to change, great things happen. When they are willing to question everything they've done to this point, we can explore new possibilities.

Consider where you are today. Are you being completely honest about your crisis? Are you willing to be fully open and transparent, ignoring nothing that pertains to healing your troubled marriage? Finally, are you willing to submit to the change process? Are you willing to follow through even if your old way of life is threatened?

Rattling Your Cage

Spouses usually want to point the finger of blame at each other. To believe our mate is responsible for our problems is safer, easier, and less painful than accepting some responsibility. We build a protective shell around ourselves and expect our mate to change to alleviate our turmoil.

"If it wasn't for her, I'd be fine," he rationalizes.

"If only he'd change, things would be perfect," she says.

Of course, this is rubbish. It's *not* all about them. In fact, it's often all about us. Our familiar default reactions haven't worked in years and aren't working now.

A marriage crisis rattles our cage. Crisis marriage counseling also rattles our cage. I recall a very unpleasant moment when our pastor stepped squarely on my toes.

"David," he said, leaning toward me. "You seem to overreact to Christie's criticisms. When she says something you don't like, you take it personally and become defensive."

I couldn't believe my pastor would talk to me this way. Aren't pastors supposed to be loving, kind, nurturing, gentle, and compassionate? And here he had the audacity to suggest I was overreacting to criticism!

Impossible, I thought. I'm a trained psychologist, familiar with the ways of the psyche.

"I can handle criticism if it's delivered to me in a fair manner," I said.

"And she's supposed to know all the rules about how to speak to you? You've had 30 years of experience. Do you really expect her to be up and running like a professional colleague in a year or two? Is that a fair playing field, or is it possible you're expecting too much?"

You could have heard a pin drop. Holy cow! Who gave this guy the right to talk to me this way? But there it was. An insight, dead on, that rattled my cage. I could either accept his feedback or throw it off and risk the consequences.

Whenever I wanted to focus on Christie's criticism, Pastor Paul told me we needed to talk about my defensiveness and my insistence on setting up the rules of engagement. Whenever I wanted to focus on Christie's faults, Pastor Paul forced me to focus on my own. Boy, did that make me squirm!

A crisis often occurs because of our tendency to view our mate as the problem. We see their faults while myopically ignoring our own. We want to rattle their cage, they want to rattle ours, and the stalemate begins.

Michele Weiner Davis, in her book *The Divorce Remedy*, speaks to this issue.

> Even if couples begin marriage with the enlightened view that there are many valid perspectives on any given situation, they tend to develop severe amnesia quickly. And rather than brainstorm creative solutions, couples often battle tenaciously to get their partners to admit they are wrong.[2]

Pointing the finger of blame doesn't work. If you want this crisis to be an opportunity for change, you must be willing to have your cage rattled. If you're dead set on seeing things the way you've always seen them, especially if it means you're the victim and your mate is the villain, you're not going to change, and the relationship will not improve.

It's Not Too Late

Sometimes we awaken with a start and wonder if we're already late. Did we miss that important meeting? Is there still time to catch the train? Or at our house, do we have time to make it to the ferry?

As you read this book, perhaps you are wondering if it's too late to save your marriage. Almost without exception, there is time. Whether you awaken and find that you have three major problems or thirty-three, this is not the issue. It's only too late to sort things out if you don't start now.

But what are some ways to wake up? Robert Pasick, in his book *Awakening from the Deep Sleep,* offers these suggestions:

- Learn to recognize when you are experiencing a feeling. Our feelings are among our surest tools for emerging from a deep sleep. We awaken to our world primarily through our feelings. Are you allowing yourself to feel all of your emotions, or do you label them as good and bad feelings?
- Identify the feeling. Turning on your "feeling button" is the first step, and learning to identify and label the feeling is the next. This is not as easy as it might sound. Many people struggle to identify whether they are feeling hurt or rejected, sad or angry, frightened or discouraged. We often experience a combination of feelings, so don't be surprised if you unearth a tangled web of emotions.
- Identify what has triggered the feeling. Feelings are attached to events and situations. Have you been hurt by harsh words? Are you feeling misunderstood? Listen to your feelings and consider the situation that triggered them.
- Communicate about your feelings to others. Yes, this step

is risky. You need to feel safe when talking about your feelings, and today that safety may not come from your mate. Nonetheless, find someone safe who will listen to your feelings nonjudgmentally.

- Identify your needs based on your feelings. Your emotions will help you assess what is happening and will also help you determine what you need. Consider that your emotions are energy-in-motion and will often direct you to a course of action. Consider what that action might be at this time of your life.[3]

Waking up to your feelings is a wonderful step toward healing. Although you might not be in a place where you can share all of them with your mate, you can prepare yourself for the time when you can share them openly and freely.

Unless the Lord Builds the House

Perhaps this book finds you with a marital house in shambles. You've been devastated by infidelity or emotional betrayal and wonder if there's anything to rebuild. You sit amid emotional and relational rubble. Can this marital house be rebuilt?

Yes.

Perhaps you're living in a marital house that's been rebuilt time and time again, and it looks like Old Mother Hubbard's shanty—ragtag, dilapidated, weakened, and weathered by time. You've heard or spoken angry words again and again, and faced crisis after crisis. You're exhausted and wonder whether your marriage can be rebuilt.

Yes.

Perhaps your marital house looks perfectly fine when you slap on a new coat of paint. You're polite as you talk to one another, but you don't trust each other with real intimacy. Beneath the facade you know that your house is rickety because it lacks a solid foundation. Can your marriage be rebuilt?

Yes.

We have a wonderful God who will help us rebuild dilapidated relationships; He'll offer wisdom and guidance as we repair the shattered foundations of our marriages.

"Unless the Lord builds the house, its builders labor in vain. Unless the Lord watches over the city, the watchmen stand guard in vain" (Psalm 127:1). We can rest in assurance that God will not fail us. "He who began a good work in you will carry it on to completion until the day of Christ Jesus" (Philippians 1:6).

These Scriptures offer great hope. Even though you are experiencing a crisis and the situation is urgent, your marriage belongs to the Lord. If you dedicate yourselves to Him and allow Him to rebuild your marriage, He can do it.

7

Eliminating Barriers to Change

When patterns are broken, new worlds emerge.

Tuli Kupferberg

I received word the other day that a Christian couple I'd worked with a year ago had recently divorced. The news saddened and shocked me.

Trish and Don were an attractive couple with two young children. Don was a chiropractor with a vibrant practice. Trish worked as his office manager. Articulate and insightful, they were on the fast track to success. They built a custom home overlooking the city and enjoyed their growing financial prosperity. They energetically pursued civic and church activities.

They came to counseling because of Trish's depression and her discouragement over Don's "irritability and control," which seemed to stem in large part from pressures he felt from his clinical practice. Trish said she felt like she was "living in a pressure cooker" and voiced regrets about marrying someone so intense. When she threatened a separation unless they received help, he complied.

Encouraged to counsel by their pastor as well, Don approached our sessions matter-of-factly. He came, he worked, and he left—often prematurely. I thought their marriage crisis would be enough to alert them to lifestyle changes that they needed to make, but this apparently was not the case.

I enjoyed working with Don and Trish, but I could sense from the beginning his resistance to counseling. He made time for the appointments at first and seemed eager to change when Trish threatened divorce, but he grew restless as we dug deeper into their issues. The more focus and commitment counseling demanded, the more he resisted. He indicated fairly quickly, "We can take what you've taught us and run with it." This is often a euphemism for, "You're starting to demand too much of me, and I'm going to opt out rather than change."

Don's irritability and control weren't their only problems. They also struggled to communicate effectively, with arguments ensuing over the smallest issues. Don tried to coerce Trish, overpowering her with sheer emotional force in an attempt to make her do things his way. When these patterns were pointed out to him, he put on the blinders. He portrayed himself as being right and pointed out that Trish ought to go along with his ways of doing things. She resisted, and when she did, eruptions occurred.

Although we made progress, I always doubted that Don's perceptions had really been altered. I feared the changes were superficial. They left counseling after he insisted they didn't need further work. Sadly, Trish caved in to his demands as she had done hundreds of times before.

Don wanted the quick fix, the easy solution, the shortcut. He didn't want to have to work hard to save his marriage, though he insisted it was very important to him. My efforts to reach him through counseling failed, and so did his marriage.

When I heard of their divorce, I wondered why they had opted for a divorce instead of returning for additional counseling. Was it pride? Was it fear of change? I'll never know.

Because I don't have the complete story, I guard against being overly critical of their decision. All I know is that Don resisted change—and I've certainly been in his shoes. As I explained in the previous chapter, there was a time when I wanted to smoke, hang out in bars, and have my shaggy Irish setters greet me at the door when I returned home.

I liked my old life. But after three or four hospitalizations, I decided that breathing was better than not breathing. After several years and a scare from a physician, I finally relented and agreed to change.

I wish I could say that my medical crisis has translated into other victories in my life and that I now find making changes a routine matter. Such is not the case. Ask my wife, Christie. I dance on the edge of calamity far too frequently.

Just the other night I awakened with a start, agitated and anxious. This seems to be my MO—I sail through my days, but when it's bedtime, the worries catch up to me. I felt as though I were pinned beneath the blankets. I lay face to face with unfinished business.

I've taken on more responsibilities recently. These obligations seemed like good choices at the time. A Sunday school class in the fall, another book contract, two speaking engagements, and a Marriage Intensive with a couple flying in from Texas. I had measured out my time and felt that I could handle these responsibilities. But now I wondered.

In a panic, I got up, grabbed my journal, and began writing. I reconsidered some of the recent additions to my schedule, evaluating which were creating the most pressure and considering ways of regaining balance. I decided to reduce the counseling load at my office, penciled in an extra day off, and scheduled a sailing date with my son.

I'm still learning to listen to my body *before* I reach crisis mode.

The Gambler

Trish and Don remind me of the gambler I discussed in the previous chapter. He decided that gambling was better than not gambling, that enjoying the thrill of the big win was better than sitting at home and doing the same old thing. His wife decided that rocking the boat was too risky and that she could live with the struggles that accompanied his addiction. So they travel a treacherous road, heading irrevocably toward another crisis.

We've all heard the alarms. We know instinctively that we're on a rocky road. Why in the world won't we heed the doctor's advice?

Why won't we listen before we're standing before a judge at a divorce hearing?

This chapter is critical to our comprehension of what it takes to really change. The key is to understand that there are natural barriers we must face and eliminate. We must learn the importance of understanding that anything short of real change is simply the equivalent of riding in a boat, caught in the rapids that will carry us to the falls. The goal of this chapter is to help you identify your barriers to change and the strategies necessary to bring those barriers down.

Denial

Much of the reason for our avoidance of change can be found in a single word: *denial.* We tolerate crises largely because of denial. We tell ourselves that things are not as bad as they seem or that they are getting better when in fact they're not. We tell ourselves we're not at fault, but in reality, we've played a major part in moving things to this crisis point.

Denial is the frog in the kettle saying, "It's really not that warm in here."

Denial is the gambler saying, "I really have control over my gambling habits."

Denial is the gambler's wife saying, "I really think he can manage his gambling this time."

Denial is me telling myself, "Smoking and drinking a little won't affect my breathing."

Denial is the couple in crisis saying, "I don't know how we got into this mess. It must be something he [or she] is doing that makes our relationship so difficult. It certainly can't be anything I'm doing wrong."

Denial tells us, "Our crisis is not really a crisis. That alarm isn't really an alarm."

Finally, denial says, "We don't really have a spiritual problem. We don't really have an emotional problem. In fact, we don't really even have a relational problem."

Denial is a powerful culprit. However, we cannot continue to deny reality if we hope to avoid another relational catastrophe. Although denial may help us feel better temporarily, in the end it often makes us feel worse. The denial we use to protect ourselves ultimately hurts us. If we are intent on making good use of the current crisis, we must emerge from our state of denial.

Relief

During a marriage crisis we are looking for an end to our pain, though not necessarily a change in the way we behave. We want the troublesome person to adjust while we may actually resist the arduous change process ourselves. Although we're often motivated to change the thing causing us distress, we also tend to avoid the change process like the plague, leaving us in a double bind.

The gambler's wife is a perfect example. She was miserable and sought my services to persuade her husband to quit gambling. But when she discovered the emotional cost needed to create change, she weakened. She quickly realized that change was not simple. I can imagine her thought process.

Relief plan A: "I can live in misery, knowing my husband will probably relapse into gambling, jeopardizing our finances."

Relief plan B: "I can insist on him entering recovery, knowing he'll put up a big fight that will create extreme tension in our marriage."

Both A and B have obvious problems. Both carry the imminent prospect of tension. Thus, the foreseeable future is fraught with significant challenges. This is why so many people opt, as she did, for another plan.

Relief plan C: "I can use denial myself, believing that he will keep his gambling under control. Maybe he'll somehow see the error of his ways, and our lives will improve."

In plan C, denial is the key ingredient. In fact, as things spin out of control, it takes more and more denial to pretend that all is well. It's hard to pretend that things will be fine when, day after day, they aren't. In his book *Dropping Your Guard,* Chuck Swindoll says this:

> It is the nature of the beast within all of us to resist change. The familiar draws us in and constrains us like a magnet. Most folks would rather stay the same and suffer than risk change and find relief. This is especially true when the future is threatening. Being creatures of habit, many would rather frown at today's familiar misery and stay in the mess than smile at tomorrow's adventure.[1]

We want relief from our marriage crises but don't want to let go of our familiar trappings. Thus, we prolong our grief.

The Shortcut

One of the greatest barriers to lasting change is an inclination to take the shortcut. We're all acquainted with the tendency to opt for the quickest, shortest path from point A to point B. Sometimes the ability to find a quicker way to do things is a sign of brilliance; sometimes it's an act of denial.

As a youth, I had a shortcut to my friend's house. I discovered I could head out my backyard, cut across the neighbor's backyard, go through the woods and end up at my buddy's house in seven or eight minutes, nearly half the time of my previous route using the street. The choice was clear—take the shortcut.

Using this same strategy in character change, however, is faulty. When I try to use shortcuts, such as settling for cosmetic solutions to my character flaws, the weaknesses always resurface in my relationships, creating significant problems.

I've discovered that I'm a master of the shortcut. I don't know whether it's a genetic defect, personality flaw, or simply a childhood trait I've carried into adulthood. I've been known (in the past!) for throwing cans out the car window instead of taking them to the trash, purposely exceeding the speed limit to get someplace faster instead of leaving early enough to make the drive at a moderate speed, and even cheating on high school exams instead of studying properly and earning honest grades. I'm not proud of these maneuvers, but I understand that they were all ways to avoid taking the long way around.

The problem with the shortcut is clear in relation to marital problems—the underlying problems are never solved, and they lead to even greater conflicts. Quick fixes don't work. Short-term solutions only last for a short time. When problems aren't solved, they rear their ugly heads again and again. Soon you have a snowball effect—a small problem becomes a giant one. A single problem is lumped together with several others, making it nearly impossible to tease the issues apart.

Pick-Up Sticks

When working with couples, I sometimes feel as if I'm playing pick-up sticks. As I listen to them describe their crises, I hear about a pile of problems. Most often, they are trying to pick up just one stick (problem) at a time without disturbing the others. As you can imagine, this is nearly impossible to do. Usually one issue touches feelings from another issue, and soon we're into a cascade of problems.

"You have layers of problems that you've denied," I tell them. "We're addressing not just one issue but years of problems that haven't been dealt with effectively. We've got to do our best to identify the problems and address them."

Couples respond to this analogy. They recognize the layers of problems even though they struggle to sort them out and place them in neat stacks. They catch themselves drifting from one dilemma to another, disrupting the entire pile along the way. I help them recognize when they are disregarding one issue and focusing exclusively on another.

"Each problem is integrally related to the others, so it's hard not to talk about everything all at once," I tell them. "But we've got to try to deal with them individually. We'll come to see that each issue is related to the other issues. When we identify these patterns, we can work on them."

Emerging from denial and facing issues that lead to marriage crises means stepping back and looking at the problems in the stack. It means labeling the problems without being overwhelmed by the immensity of the pile. It means working very hard to discuss one issue at a time and to keep the slate of problems clean.

Facing the Truth

When we contemplate the pile of sticks (problems) before us, we are tempted to grab one and attack it viciously, bringing down the entire stack. This lack of finesse and sensitivity only adds to the problems, creating a larger mess.

"I'm just telling the truth," one man said to me recently.

"Yes," I replied, "but that truth hurts. What happened to the love part?"

"Do I have to tiptoe in what I say?" he answered abruptly.

"Sometimes, yes. Your wife is very sensitive, and a strong word can feel very hurtful to her. A soft word, saying the same thing, will do just fine."

It's also tempting to focus on a single stick while ignoring the rest. Sometimes we are like dogs with a bone, grabbing onto an issue and not letting it rest—all in the name of speaking the truth. We grab onto a stick and won't let go.

This analogy applies to our marriage crises and the prospect of change. Your situation demands that you step back and face the truth of the matter, as uncomfortable as that may be. It demands that you face the truth by gaining perspective about how many sticks (problems) there are, which ones are yours and which ones are your partner's, what you can do about your issues and what your mate needs to do about his or her issues.

Navigating a marriage crisis means methodically eliminating your defensiveness, replacing your underlying denial with honesty, and picking up the sticks one by one. It means having a mind-set that says...

"I'm open to learning about how I'm contributing to this problem."

"I want to hear the truth from you about what I'm like to live with."

"I'm open to your suggestions about how I might change to make our marriage better."

"I'm willing to listen to other professionals speak into my life about my problems."

This is no easy task. To lower your defenses and invite feedback is difficult. Eliminating barriers to change is not for the faint of heart. But it is absolutely necessary, as Patricia Love, in her book *The Truth About Love,* says:

> The truth about love is ever changing. Throughout the life of a relationship, individuals change and life itself changes. Love has to be flexible enough to accommodate new information, new roles, and new ways of loving one another. Most low spots in relationships occur out of a need for discovery. If couples do not make a practice of examining current needs and making adjustments, they get stuck in a rut that offers little or no reward.[2]

Most challenges in relationships occur because couples have failed to take in new information. They haven't been diligent about seeking the truth, as painful as it might be.

Are you willing to dedicate yourself to discovering the truth about your marriage? Will you be meticulous in exploring the underlying reasons for your current crisis? This will require a great deal of courage on your part, but the result can be immensely rewarding.

Breaking Through the Barriers

Change demands a lot from us. It requires breaking out of established patterns that inevitably lead to marriage crises. It requires letting go of old ways of seeing things and abandoning failed methods of dealing with problems. As Dr. Love said, we must be willing to explore our issues from new angles. We must be willing to face the truth about our problems. Shortcuts and quick fixes don't work. Real change involves real commitment, effort, and engagement. Here are some practical tools for breaking through your barriers to change:

1. Begin to own your stuff. Owning your stuff means recognizing that you've created the mess you're in. It doesn't work to hide behind the belief that the problem is somewhere "out there" rather than somewhere "in here." The only person you can change is you, and the only stuff you can really work on is the stuff you bring to the table.

2. Begin with yourself. You will be tempted to focus on what your mate is doing wrong, but if you do, you will only spin your wheels. Focusing on your mate prevents you from moving forward. Traction in solving your problems comes from looking in the mirror for ways to change.

3. Determine precisely what to do. Vague goals and lofty dreams are just that—vague and lofty. A concrete plan for change is essential. Precisely what are you going to change, and how will you know if you've been successful? Who's going to hold you accountable for this change? Breaking through the barriers means establishing practical steps you are willing to take to become the person God and your mate want you to be.

4. Commit to be humble. Humility comes from the Latin word *humilis,* meaning low, humble, of earth (hence the English word *humus*). We'll never be honest with ourselves about changes we must make while maintaining a pretentious attitude. The 12-step program of Alcoholics Anonymous promotes taking a moral inventory of how we've hurt others with our behavior. Considering how our actions have affected our mate is a great way to begin the process of change.

5. Make a commitment. None of us are perfect, and we have an incredible tendency to shift back into our familiar misery, so we must commit ourselves to trying again and again. We cannot allow ourselves to wallow in discouragement, nor can we afford to take half measures when it comes to change. We must count the cost and then commit ourselves to action.

Another critical element that fuels commitment is our heartfelt belief that the path we're taking is the right one for us. Any efforts coming from external motivations are likely to fail, while efforts made from a deep conviction are likely to be sustained.

6. Rely on God. Who among us hasn't vowed to change under our own power, only to drop in our tracks halfway through the race? We need the transforming power of God in order to be honest with ourselves about our shortcomings and to sustain the effort needed to really change.

Chris Thurman sets us straight on the power of the ego to make these lasting changes: "Personal power, as much as it gets held in high esteem in our culture, isn't enough to bring about deep, lasting change."[3] The true source of power for lasting change comes from God.

Consider the words of King David as he faced the transforming power of God's love in the human heart: "I know my transgressions, and my sin is always before me. Against you, and you only, have I sinned and done what is evil in your sight, so that you are proved right when you speak and justified when you judge" (Psalm 51:3). Breaking the barriers of change begins and ends with truth in our inner parts—and allowing God to transform us.

Metanoia

What does it mean to allow God to change us, and how does this happen? Personally, I'm very impatient with this process and not at all certain that I'm ever completely allowing God to do His transforming work in me.

Superficial, white-knuckle alteration may help a little, but deep transformation is better. The Scriptures deal extensively with the concept of change, and when they do, the passage invariably involves the transformation of the entire person.

Metanoia is a Greek word meaning a change of mind. Jesus preached about this type of inward transformation: a radical revision and transformation of our entire mental process. In this change of mind, God takes center stage in our hearts and minds. The apostle Paul says we can be transformed by the renewing of our minds (Romans 12:2; Ephesians 4:23).

Metanoia means creating a new mind. It involves allowing the grace of God to enter into our lives and teach us how to see our true selves. It involves change from the inside out rather than from the outside in. It involves the Holy Spirit entering our hearts and literally transforming the way we think, the way we see the world, and most importantly, the way we relate to ourselves and others.

Our minds are also changed by God changing our circumstances. For some He has to grab our complete attention: The apostle Paul spent three years in Arabia, Moses spent forty years in the desert, and Joseph spent thirteen years in Egypt.

When transformed from within by the Holy Spirit, we let go of the struggle to change, and we allow God to do His work. Convicted by the Spirit, we allow God to work on parts of our character that need to be changed. Submitting to the power of the Spirit, we no longer anxiously strive to change. Instead, we allow the Spirit to work within us. Still, we are responsible to do our part. As we immerse ourselves in Scripture reading, prayer, and meditation, the Word dwells richly in us and transforms us (Colossians 3:16).

The apostle Paul offers this depiction of the miraculous change process:

> So I say, live by the Spirit, and you will not gratify the desires of the sinful nature. For the sinful nature desires what is contrary to the Spirit, and the Spirit what is contrary to the sinful nature...But the fruit of the Spirit is love, joy, peace, patience, kindness, goodness, faithful, gentleness and self-control. Against such things there is no law (Galatians 5:16-23).

8

Strengthening the Positive

He has made everything beautiful in its time.
He has also set eternity in the hearts of men.
Ecclesiastes 3:11

Finding anything good to focus on is difficult when you're in the midst of a marriage crisis. Waves of emotion create a gulf between you and your mate. With your emotional bridge in shambles, seeing the other side can be tough.

Steven is a bright lawyer who is married to Sarah, a winsome young woman. I began working with them after a severe crisis in their marriage prompted them to call for an emergency appointment.

Steven and Sarah are both in their early thirties and have three children. They came to see me after Steven had an affair with his personal assistant at his law firm. The affair, which he readily admitted after being discovered, devastated both of them.

"I never thought I'd do something like this," Steven said with obvious disgust.

"And I never thought you'd be capable of it either," Sarah said. "I thought we had so much going for us, but I guess not. If you could do this, we don't have anything."

Sarah was obviously filled with anger and needed to vent. I waited for her to continue.

"I asked Steven to leave last week," she said. "We have nothing if we don't have trust. I'm not sure if there's even any purpose in us coming to counseling. What's the point? I'm not sure if I want to be married to a man with so little self-control."

Steven threw his hands up in the air and looked at me.

"I hope you can talk some sense into her," he said. "She's got me painted as a criminal. It's not like I'm denying what I did. It was wrong and I know it. But it's not like there's nothing worth salvaging here."

"You don't get it," Sarah snapped. "Anyone who can cheat on his wife and children obviously doesn't think much of his marriage. So I'm not real interested in hearing about all that we've got to salvage."

I listened to their troubling story, attempting to help each understand the other and offering hope that we'd be able to stabilize their marriage if they were willing. I discussed strategies for creating safety, which we've talked about in previous chapters. However, our session ended too quickly, and I was skeptical that they believed they could find anything worth saving.

Sarah and Steven left my office discouraged. She was weary from trying to understand how her husband could cheat on her. She was furious, but she was also frightened that he might cheat again. She felt fragile and wounded, unsure of how she would manage their three children without his help if she left him.

Steven also wondered if their marriage could be saved. I scheduled additional sessions with them and also agreed to meet with Sarah alone to help her consider her options and determine how best to cope with this emergency.

A Salvage Project

Sarah is extremely disheartened and sees nothing to salvage in their relationship. She sees only more trouble on the horizon. Is she right? Is there nothing to salvage? Is it time for her to walk away? Many people in her circumstances do just that. However, it's important to consider the possibilities when the problem is fixable. Acting impulsively is rarely the best choice.

An exciting movement is taking place in many of our urban areas. In Seattle and Tacoma, close to where I reside, run-down warehouses are being transformed into chic, modern loft condominiums. Worn brick facades are being sandblasted and restored to their original beauty. What was once on the short list for demolition is now being targeted for renovation.

Someone had the insight to see the possibilities in these industrial sections of town, once considered to be a blight on the urban landscape. Now, after standing empty for many years, these classic buildings are bustling with boutiques, salons, day spas, and luxury apartments.

Rather than focusing on the problems, developers and designers saw the possibilities. They looked beyond the rust and rubble to the distinctive lines and patina.

My wife has that kind of eye. Christie can see beyond the obvious and into the possibility. She can integrate the potential into the problem. Recently, she excitedly asked if I'd go with her to see an old barge located in a marina not far from our home.

"Why do we want to see an old barge?" I said.

"Because it has possibilities. I saw a picture of it and noticed that it had wonderful lines and lots of interior room. It could be something."

"What do you mean?"

"I just mean it could be something. I don't know what it could be. You have to keep an open mind."

Keeping an Open Mind

An open mind? For a couple in crisis, this is like swimming across the Amazon River without fear of crocodiles and piranhas. When danger signs are everywhere, keeping an open mind goes against every instinct. Fleeing seems like a more reasonable option.

Sarah didn't want to keep an open mind. She wanted to form a kangaroo court right then and there, haul in her husband and the other woman, and find them guilty. She had no desire for patience, tolerance, or understanding.

To keep an open mind is nearly impossible when your relationship is held together by a thread, when you feel angry, hurt, and misunderstood. With emotions running rampant, insight and wisdom are in short supply.

To her credit, Sarah came back for counseling. She struggled, however, with many challenging questions:

Did his affair really mean there was nothing to salvage?

What positive qualities in their marriage could she still count on?

Was her husband likely to repeat his infidelity?

How could she show her love for him when she was so angry and hurt by his behavior?

Your crisis might be different from Steven and Sarah's. Perhaps you're not struggling with sexual unfaithfulness. Perhaps you're besieged by a lack of safety in your marriage, a lack of emotional warmth and affection, or an atmosphere of bitterness and hostility that never seems to abate.

You may be struggling as much as Sarah to keep an open mind. Being hurt again and again creates an environment of antagonism and animosity, and you've begun to see your mate in a negative light. You're in a crisis, and you've lost the ability to remember the good things about your marriage.

Remember

When a marriage is flooded with negative emotions, as is the case during most crises, we forget the good qualities that attracted us to our mate in the first place. Our positive feelings are obliterated by so many hurts and hurdles that we can hardly find our way back to where we once were. We distance ourselves from the positive feelings in order to survive. This is a natural aspect of denial.

The good news is that the positive feelings are often still there, but they're buried beneath the ruin of harsh words, degrading actions, and distant demeanor. We become separated from what has been good and vibrant in our marriage, and now, striving to maintain an open mind, we must remember. We must reattach ourselves to those wonderful qualities that currently lay dormant. These positive feelings, often razor thin, can help form the foundation of the bridge that allows us to find our way back to our mate.

Just like those designers and visionaries who looked at the aged buildings in downtown Seattle and Tacoma and saw vibrant shops, lofts, cafes, and walking malls, you must work hard to remember the beauty that lies beneath the ashes in your marriage. Rather than rehearsing the pain that screams, "There's nothing left to save," you must force yourself to remember and reconnect yourself to the good that lies buried in the hidden places of your marriage.

When I met with Sarah for several individual sessions, I encouraged her to vent her enormous pain. Her loss was immense: the innocence of young love and a seemingly perfect family; betrayal by the man she'd held in high regard; the endless, sordid pictures in her mind of her husband being with another woman; having to explain to their children why their daddy was no longer living in their home. Her pain was great, her loss overwhelming.

But hidden in the debris of that pain were possibilities. I asked her to do something she didn't want to do—remember.

I asked Sarah to tell me about their marriage, how they'd met, the activities they'd enjoyed as a family, and the qualities that had made her happy to be Steven's wife. She initially flinched when asked to do so—it was far easier to stay enraged and wounded with her pain serving as a protective barrier. If she could stay furious, perhaps she'd never be hurt like this again. Unfortunately, she would also forfeit the possibility of salvaging a loving marriage. She'd relinquish the opportunity to learn how and why this had happened and what she could do to lessen the likelihood of it occurring again. She'd give up the possibility of having a deeper, richer marriage than she thought possible.

Sarah softened during her third session. I'd sent her away from the previous meeting with instructions to write down at least five reasons she decided to marry Steven. Her list was exactly what I'd hoped to see.

> He was a kind, gentle man, sympathetic to those in need.
>
> He had a great sense of humor and was always witty and ready to have fun.
>
> He was bright and able to carry on genuine conversations.
>
> He was determined. He wanted to do something with his life.
>
> He wanted a family and was a caring husband and father.
>
> He took responsibility for his failures.

"How many of these qualities still exist?" I asked.

"I'm not sure," she replied. "The Steven I know is gone. I don't know this guy."

"You talk as if Steven is no longer himself, as though he's turned into some monster with a split personality."

"Those are my thoughts exactly: some kind of monster. That's the only way I can explain what happened."

"I think that's your hurt and anger speaking, Sarah. You can't decide if he is still a sensitive man. You don't know if he still has a good sense of humor. You don't think he still wants his family more than anything. But I think both of us know that's not the case."

"Nothing can justify what he did."

"What he did was horrible," I said. "No question. But can you honestly say he doesn't still have the qualities you cared about in the beginning?"

Sarah began to cry uncontrollably.

"He hurt me so bad," she said. "How could he do that to me? I've loved him completely. I didn't deserve this."

"No, you didn't," I said. "And it will be incredibly difficult to move past this. You need to realize that some things will challenge you as you try to deal with this. Some aspects of the marriage may have played a role in his affair."

"Are you saying I caused this?" she snapped.

"Of course not," I said. "But you'll need to keep an open mind when it comes to understanding the factors that played a role in his poor choice."

"I'm just afraid we've lost everything and that we'll never be able to get it back."

"I've worked with hundreds of couples in this situation, Sarah, and many are able to rebuild their marriages. If they can keep an open mind, they discover that the man or woman they fell in love with is still there. In your case, Steven wants to make things right. He wants to make amends, learn how and why this happened, and do everything humanly possible to make sure it never happens again."

"Maybe," Sarah said. "I'd like to believe we could patch our lives back together."

"Will you do your best to remember the qualities you've always loved about Steven? I'd like you to read your list to me again and imagine that they still exist."

After many counseling sessions, Sarah began to understand that the things she loved about Steven were still there and available to her—if she would allow the healing to begin.

Reaching for the Positive

Remembering anything positive is challenging in the midst of broken trust, violated safety and stability, and painful emotions. Everything can appear bleak. That's the nature of crises. Perceptions are skewed, emotions are frayed and edgy, and the outlook appears dismal.

In the midst of this desperation, however, opportunity awaits. There is a chance to remember what was good about your mate before the crisis and what still can be grasped within the relationship today and in the future. You can look clearly at the situation and determine if a reasonable risk is worth taking.

Sarah could begin remembering many positive traits about Steven, but to do so she'd have to decide if Steven was worth the risk, and that would require an open mind, a strong dose of wisdom, and immense courage.

We explored some of her memories of what they had built as a couple. Stretching beyond her comfort zone, beyond the ever-present hurt, she began to see some of their legacy:

three lovely children: Brianne (age three), Chelsea (age five), and Tyler (age nine)

several years of teaching young married couples in their church

a beautiful country home where they bred Arabian horses

a large extended family—hers and his

many wonderful vacations, including a favorite at a small coastal village in Mexico

a vibrant church family

a shared enjoyment of movies, the theater, and community activities

a strong and enduring attraction to one another

Sarah smiled faintly as she reviewed the life she had built with Steven. She still loved his company and longed to plan another vacation to the village they enjoyed so much in Mexico. She missed seeing him walk down to the barn in his suit and knee-high boots to water and feed their horses. She missed sitting with him in church and gathering their children for their Sunday afternoon pizza ritual. She missed her old life.

"But that's all gone now," Sarah said wistfully. "He ruined it. It will never be the same."

"No, Sarah," I said. "Right now, that life is covered with the pain of his affair, but much of what you've built is still there. If you want—but only if you want—you can remember, recapture, and reattach yourself to many aspects of your old life."

"And what about what he's done to dirty our relationship?"

"I guess it's like the old barge my wife had me look at a few weeks ago. It had a lot of stains, some broken hinges on doors, and some window caulking that needed to be replaced. But it's got great lines and immense possibilities. My wife says it can be brought back to its glory years with some elbow grease."

"Maybe you're right," Sarah said slowly.

"I think for now, 'maybe' is a wise choice. No 'forevers' until we see why he did what he did and whether he's willing to do some work to make sure it never happens again."

What We Focus On

I watched Sarah's disposition and perspective change slightly over a few weeks. She changed what she focused on and the meaning she attached to the horrific events. She began to open her mind to new possibilities.

Sarah reminded me that when we focus on something, we magnify its importance. In fact, what we see becomes our reality. In the midst of a crisis, we focus on the harsh words, the disdainful glances, the withdrawn love. Reeling in pain, we focus on those agonizing aspects of the relationship.

Couples in crisis lose sight of the positive elements in their marriage. Because they feel so much pain and because they dwell on that pain, they can't enjoy the positive aspects of the relationship that still exist.

"I know I still love him," Sarah said to me recently, "but I'm so angry with him at times that I can't feel that love."

"How do you know you still love him?" I asked.

"I just know that I do," she said. "I don't really want to lose him. He's brought me such joy during our marriage."

"It does sound to me like you love him. Maybe part of the issue is what you focus on."

"What do you mean?"

"What we focus on tends to become magnified," I said. "It's like a dog with a bone. First, the dog has the bone. After a while, the bone has the dog. The dog thinks he's so smart when he gets the bone. But after a while, he's still holding onto the bone and there's no meat left on the thing."

She laughed, nodding in recognition.

"We can be like that when it comes to marriage," I continued. "We cling to old feelings instead of allowing new ones to enter the picture. We need to allow ourselves time and space to grieve, to be sure, but we must also allow positive feelings to return."

"Are you saying that when I constantly think and talk about my anger toward him, that anger becomes bigger?"

"Not only that, but you lose the opportunity to feel other emotions, like joy, love, kindness, and gratefulness."

Sarah and Steven have a chance to save their marriage, but they have a lot of work to do. They'll have to decide if they want to weather this storm or start over on their own. Time will tell, but for today it looks like they have an opportunity to start rebuilding their relationship.

The Bad-Day Blues

Have you ever had a bad day and then allowed it to overwhelm you? Many times our situation is not as terrible as it feels at the moment.

Many of us allow our emotions to take over and cloud our judgment. As a result, the problems escalate to the point where they seem insurmountable. Psychologists call this *catastrophizing*—taking a normal, troubling situation and blowing it out of proportion to the point where it is much worse.

Judith Viorst, author of the delightful book *Alexander and the Terrible, Horrible, No Good, Very Bad Day,* caused us all to laugh and think when she introduced us to Alexander, a kid with one problem on top of another. Alexander had a negative cloud hanging over his head, and nothing ever seemed to go his way.

Alexander is like us in many ways. From the moment he awakens, he's met with trouble. Nothing goes right, and he develops a sour attitude, expecting more problems to befall him. He wakes up with gum in his hair, and unlike his brothers he has no prize in his morning cereal. Hoping for better luck, he wants to move to Australia—the land down under—where things might be upside down and bad luck will turn to good luck.

As we read of Alexander's misfortunes, we can't help but smile. Is it because we've all been there? We've all had days and weeks when things didn't go our way. We've had times, perhaps even seasons, when we've sulked and counted our problems instead of our blessings. We recognize Alexander's myopia—his tendency to focus on his problems while ignoring things that might actually be going his way.

How is Alexander's story applicable to a marriage in crisis? During marriage crises, everyone else's life can appear better, smoother, happier, and kinder than our own. We may even believe our mate is having an easier go of it. We sulk, cry, and become agitated, all the while forgetting to notice the good things that may be happening. We see only the bad—and the bad becomes intensified. Before we know it, an entrenched bad mood gains momentum as we rehearse what's not going our way.

Can we let go of our negative thinking? Of course, but doing so takes practice. Instead of rehearsing all the things that aren't going our way, obsessing on the aspects of our marriage that trouble us, how about trying the following?

Identify things about your mate that you still appreciate.

Refuse to spend hours arguing and bickering.

Agree to share with your mate the traits you still appreciate about each other.

Stop rehearsing marital problems.

Seek and discuss solutions to the problems.

Bad days are part of life. But they don't need to become a way of life. Severe marriage crises happen, but there are often ways to get past them. Accentuating the positive and minimizing the negative will help you to that end.

Although Alexander is cute and our hearts go out to him, another part of us wants to sit him down for a lecture:

"Look, Alexander, life doesn't have to be as bad as you make it. When you focus on the prizes you're *not* getting, you lose sight of the ones you *are* getting. When you count all the things you've lost, you miss out on all the things you've gained. It's time to get on with life."

Bad moods and bad days come with the territory. But bad weeks, months, and years are often optional.

Empathy

A critical barrier between a couple in crisis is the perpetrator/victim mind-set, which can be a serious impediment to healing. Here's how it goes: Having perceived myself as getting a raw deal from you, I rehearse the wrongs I've suffered and remind myself again and again that I am the victim. Of course, this point of view narrows my vision and causes me to move further and further away from you because I blame you for the pain I'm feeling.

Without intervention, before long I've convinced myself that you can never be trusted, you can never satisfy my needs, and you can never help me. In fact, you're completely toxic, and I need to get away from you. Can you see the harm in taking such a position?

The odd thing is that your mate is probably having the same thoughts about you. You're the perpetrator, the victimizer who can never, never be trusted. The barriers between partners becomes larger, the gap wider, and chances of reconciliation smaller.

Rarely is one person solely the perpetrator, while the other is exclusively the victim. More often, both partners have learned to hurl insults and hurts, and both have learned to rehearse their suffering.

What's the answer?

Harville Hendrix, in his book *Getting the Love You Want,* offers some very practical solutions:

- You realize that your love relationship has a hidden purpose—the healing of childhood wounds. Yes, marriage can be a wonderful place of healing for both of you. You can have a "corrective emotional experience" where you are treated differently and better than you were in childhood.

- You create a more accurate image of your partner. You stop viewing your mate as an evil perpetrator, and begin seeing him or her as very human and fallible, just like you.
- You take responsibility for communicating your needs and desires to your partner. You must let go of the belief that your mate can read your mind, or that his or her sole job is to satisfy your needs. With your help, however, your partner will likely work on meeting your legitimate needs.
- You become more intentional in your interactions. Rather than slipping into old default patterns of interacting, you work on being proactive—planning in advance how you will react to challenging situations.
- You learn to value your partner's needs and wishes as highly as you value your own. In the mature, Christian marriage, you are willing to forego being the center of the world and strive to meet your mate's needs. In fact, you frequently stop to consider his or her immediate need, and if possible, you do your best to meet it.[1]

If you can nurture a spirit of "we're in this together and must find our solutions together" as you navigate this crisis, you'll be greatly strengthened for the journey. If you can view your mate as vulnerable, fragile, and in need of your love, you'll grow in empathy toward each other, creating a powerful bridge. And if you empathize with each other, rather than fighting, you'll be available to assist each other in the healing process.

Our Mate's Healer

Have you considered that one of your most powerful tools for finding your way through a marriage crisis will be to see yours as instrumental in your mate's healing? This may seem like a radical concept in light of the fact that you may consider your mate the instrument of your pain. Trust me, he or she doesn't want to hurt you. Your partner doesn't orchestrate each day to bring pain into your life. People who are hurting usually end up hurting others.

What if, instead of taking a position *against* each other, you took a position *for* each other? What if, during this crisis, when things look bleak and discouraging, you decide to be an instrument of healing—your mate's healing?

We are told in the creation story that Eve was created to be a helper suitable for Adam (Genesis 2:18). Although the Genesis account doesn't explain precisely how this will play out, the apostle Paul offers many illustrations of the husband-wife relationship. He instructs us to encourage one another, bearing with one another in love (Ephesians 4:2). We are to let no unwholesome word come from our mouth and to build one another up according to their needs (Ephesians 4:29). What if we offered encouragement to our mate, even in the midst of struggle and conflict?

Dr. Hendrix elaborates on this process of utilizing the marriage relationship as an instrument of healing:

> We make a decision to act on the information we are acquiring about ourselves and our partner and become our partner's healers. We go against our instinct to focus on our own needs and make a conscious choice to focus on theirs. To do this, we must conquer our fear of change. As we respond to our partner's needs, we are surprised to discover that, in healing our partner, we are slowly reclaiming parts of our own lost selves."[2]

Could this excruciating marriage crisis actually be a crucible for change and growth? Can we use this struggle to shift our focus, accentuate the positive, and step forward as a healer for our mate? Rather than viewing our mate as enemy number one, we can choose to recognize his or her wounds and assist in healing. This increases the likelihood that our partner will assist us in healing as well.

Plugged In to the Power

The only danger in the prospect of healing our mate and in the process of being healed ourselves is in believing we can do this under our own power. The mind is willing, but the spirit is weak. We so easily slip into worn-out, default patterns of behavior. When the chips are down and we're feeling puny, to revert back to our old, hurtful ways is incredibly tempting.

What we need is a Spirit transfusion. We need to be changed from the inside out so that we learn to act from a renewed and transformed mind (Romans 12:2). With this renewed mind, controlled by God, we live out the fruit of the Spirit: love, joy, peace, patience, kindness, goodness, faithfulness, gentleness, and self-control (Galatians 5:22). Our heart literally changes toward our mate—we want to become an instrument of healing.

If you're ready for radical change, consider this suggestion by David Clarke, author of *A Marriage After God's Own Heart:*

> Reading and studying the Bible together will bring down walls and reveal who you really are. God's word will cut through every defense and barrier...Genuine closeness between a husband and wife comes only after their hearts are revealed—when they express their real thoughts, motivations, and emotions.[3]

Today, if you are embittered and angry, feeling cheated and betrayed, consider that you can undergo successful heart surgery. Through the power of God, you can change this crisis into opportunity. With a renewed heart you'll see your mate in a new light and realize that the person with whom you're angry needs encouragement from you. If you offer it, more likely than not, you'll receive healing in return.

9

Mastering the Skills

Satisfaction lies in the effort, not the attainment. Full effort is full victory.

MAHATMA GHANDI

The medic in the back of the ambulance didn't panic when the woman fractured her hip. He knew the exact course of action and took it. He'd done so many times. With increasing confidence, he'd mastered his trade and could predict the positive outcome.

I've watched the same transformation in my oldest son, Joshua, as he's grown from a frightened medical student to a self-confident doctor. Although just getting started, he's well on his way to becoming an accomplished physician.

His younger brother, Tyson, is just beginning his medical rotations. Although only two years apart, they are separated by a world of experience. Tyson hasn't endured late-night catastrophes in the emergency room; Josh has. Tyson hasn't performed emergency C-sections or routine hernia operations; Josh has.

In the same way, I don't panic when a woman calls, frantically telling me she can no longer remain in a troubled marriage.

"I can't live like this anymore," she says, her sobs intermittently interrupting her words. "Something has to change."

"I can help," I say calmly. "I can teach you skills that will guarantee you never have to go through this type of marriage emergency again."

She probably comprehends the role of an emergency room doctor to a greater degree than she understands the role of an "emergency room" psychologist. The skills, however, aren't all that different. One works to make corrections and adjustments in the body, adding medications when appropriate. The psychologist critically inspects the behaviors and thinking patterns that have created a crisis and then seeks to change them.

People have said that practice makes perfect. Others have added that *perfect* practice makes perfect. Experience alone won't give you self-confidence, but perfect practical experience can be life-changing.

There is one crucial difference between medical and psychological emergencies. After leaving the emergency room, you can relax in convalescence, allowing your body to heal. But after leaving the office of an emergency repair psychologist, you're in for the challenge of a lifetime. You will be challenged to undo entrenched patterns of behavior that led to the crisis, and you'll need to continue learning the skills necessary to prevent a marriage crisis from recurring.

If you've faced your marriage crisis head-on and are determined to create safety and security in your relationship, if you're earnest about eliminating barriers to change, and if you're ready to learn powerful, transformational skills, then you are ready to set a course toward vital, enriched marital living.

Self-Confidence

What's the primary difference between being a medical student and a physician? Experience and self-confidence.

Those two years of experience that separate my sons make a world of difference. Tyson wears a white coat but is not allowed to do anything without supervision. Because Joshua has obtained his medical degree, he is qualified to perform many medical procedures on his own.

Experience and self-confidence make a world of difference, and these two empowering assets can be yours as well. As you become more comfortable and adept at using your new skills, you'll develop the self-confidence that will help you ease out of your embittered marital crisis and into a world of loving interactions.

Practicing the additional tools discussed in this chapter will move you from crisis mode to healthy-relating mode, giving you the power to anticipate problems, head them off, and move confidently into healthier ways of relating.

I remember the first time I appeared on live television—*At Home LIVE* with Chuck and Jenni Borsellino. Already anxious because of getting lost on my way out of Dallas, I had no idea what to expect. As I was escorted to the green room, where makeup was applied and the stage director reviewed my place in the program, I began to worry about forgetting my lines, forgetting the content of my book, and perhaps even saying something off the wall that would end my brief career as a writer.

As we walked onto the set, the stage director, associate producer, camera people, and producer moved around with ease and obvious confidence. They directed guests and hosts to their seats, shouted last-minute instructions, and orchestrated the proceedings with aplomb. Meanwhile, I was scared stiff.

With nerves dancing and thoughts racing, I tried to remain calm. What would they ask me? Could I answer in a manner that would impress the hosts and the listening audience? Or would I fumble around, muddle my words, and give them the "deer in the headlights" look? I prayed like never before that I would survive the show with my ego intact.

Fortunately, everything went well.

The hosts asked questions about my book, and I was able to speak clearly about what I had written. Experience had led to confidence. I did fine that first time, and now I face television cameras and microphones with excitement and ease, thoroughly enjoying the experience.

This same confidence can be yours. Marriage crises and the problems leading to them happen for predictable reasons. If these problems are predictable, they are also preventable. If we can outline the specific issues that led to marital breakdown—and we surely can—we can prescribe a different course of action that will lead to a much more positive outcome.

This requires learning new skills, practicing those skills, and gaining proficiency at using them. As you practice, your self-confidence will grow, and you'll be able to navigate potential crisis points in the future.

The Mind-Set

Your attitude toward learning is everything. Studies consistently show that an inquisitive mind is highly correlated with intelligence. More importantly, it's also directly correlated with learning. And that's what this book is all about—learning new skills to eliminate marriage emergencies. You know that if you keep doing things the same old way, you're going to keep getting the same old results, eventually leading to crisis.

Before we can talk about new skills, however, we need to make sure you have an attitude that can assimilate new information. This is critical. Exactly how would this attitude look?

Nondefensiveness

Learning means change, and each of us has a protective barrier to learning called *defensiveness.* We know this is an incredible impediment to change, and in the last chapter we talked about having an open mind to new information. This bears repeating because of its importance.

Although defensiveness protects us, in the long run it stops us from making self-corrective changes. Emergency marriage treatment demands that we eliminate defensiveness by becoming open and receptive to learning about ourselves and the skills we must develop.

The defensive mind says, "This is not about me, but about you," but the nondefensive mind says, "I need to understand the part I've played in these problems."

The defensive mind says, "I want to focus on your faults," but the nondefensive mind says, "It's time to focus on my faults because they're the only ones I can change."

A defensive mind says, "I didn't do anything that bad," but the nondefensive mind says, "I need to know what I've done, regardless of how bad it might be."

The defensive mind says, "Quick. Give me the bottom line, and let's take a shortcut to change." But the nondefensive mind says, "I'm ready to listen attentively. I'll take the time to understand the depth of the problem."

The defensive mind says, "I hate change," but the nondefensive mind says, "I know this is all about learning and growing, so let's get on with it."

In short, nondefensiveness leads to an attitude of receptivity, which leads to change. The receptive mind is ready, willing, and able to learn new skills.

Defensiveness simply does not work, as you may have learned already. It only leads to relationship crises and disasters. Isn't it time for a change?

Embracing Criticism

Another essential attitude adjustment includes embracing criticism. No one wants to hear bad news, but leaning into bad news is always better than pretending it doesn't exist.

If you were to hear a clanking sound in the engine of your car, my hunch is that you wouldn't ignore it. As a matter of fact, you'd probably listen more closely. You'd make plans to get the car into an auto repair shop as soon as possible. Why? Because you know that the problem is only going to get worse if you ignore it.

What if you approached your marriage problems the same way? What if, instead of trying to sweep things under the rug, you listened more carefully to them? What if, instead of minimizing the impact the problems were having on your marriage, you demanded that they be addressed? Together with your mate you could "speak the truth in love" (Ephesians 4:15).

Criticism, viewed correctly, can be seen as an opportunity. If you want to bowl your mate over with surprise, invite criticism by asking, "How am I doing? Are there any issues you've not fully shared with me?" Imagine the possibilities—you're giving your mate permission to share his or her heart, noting that you want not only to hear your partner's concerns but also to deal with them effectively.

Realistic Optimism

Finally, every marriage crisis needs a strong infusion of optimism. An attitude of optimism conveys to your mate, "We can get through this. There is no problem we cannot overcome."

Imagine telling your mate that you're prepared to take this crisis very seriously, you are willing to do the hard work necessary to overcome the problems, and you believe in your ability to surmount these problems. Self-confidence gives you the power to believe that this crisis can be a learning experience.

When you're optimistic, you believe in possibilities you cannot yet see. The apostle Paul tells us that "in all things God works for the good of those who love him, who have been called according to his purpose" (Romans 8:28). Although we cannot see the final outcome, we trust that the crisis presents possibilities.

Rosamund and Ben Zander, in their delightful bestseller *The Art of Possibility,* promote seeing problems as opportunities.

> We start from what is, not from what should be; we encompass contradictions, painful feelings, fears and imaginings, and—without fleeing, blaming or attempting correction—we learn to soar, like the far-seeing hawk, over the whole landscape. The practice of being with the way things are allows us to alight in a place of openness, where "the truth" readies us for the next step, and the sky opens up.[1]

So as you employ the skills you've learned in the past few chapters, set any defensive attitude aside, eliminate barriers and resistance to change, and embrace these new ideas. Putting these skills into motion will eliminate your immediate crisis and make a tremendous difference in your marriage.

With these potent attitudes firmly in place, let's explore some of the skills needed to move beyond the present crisis.

Basic Skills

Ninety-five percent of emergency problems in a marriage can be attributed to conflicts in one of three areas: the way we listen, the way we speak, or the way we behave. A serious problem in one or more of these categories will inevitably lead to a crisis in your relationship.

Because you control each of these three areas, the prognosis is extremely good that you can make critical improvements in your marriage—provided that you are diligent and focused.

Tammie and Dale's struggle in each of these areas led to a crisis in their marriage. Referred by friends, this middle-aged couple was obviously distressed.

Fifty-five years old, Tammie walked slowly into my office, neatly dressed but obviously overweight. I had overheard her voicing criticism about our office forms with my office assistant, and before sitting down she was quick to comment that I was several minutes late for our appointment.

Dale seemed equally irritable. Wearing jeans, a baseball cap, and work boots, he appeared tired and drawn.

"Probably a waste of time for us to be here," Tammie said.

"Why do you say that?" I asked.

"Too much water under the bridge," she replied. "I doubt that you're a miracle worker, but that's what we'll need to pull this thing out of the fire. We're ready to give up on thirty years of marriage."

"Tell me about what brought you to this place in your relationship."

Tammie glanced at Dale and then began directing the session.

"Why don't you tell him why we're here," she said sharply.

"Because of your temper, you mean?" Dale said.

"Buddy, I'm tame compared to the way you talk to me! Don't try to get people to believe I'm the one with the anger problem!"

Dale smiled at me as if he'd caught his wife in the act.

"Hold it, folks," I said. "You're already going at each other, and we've hardly started."

"We can't talk about anything without it turning into an explosion," Tammie said. "I can get nasty. I admit it. But don't think Dale can't get just as mean."

"Would you agree with that, Dale? Do you get mean as well?"

"I don't start anything," Dale said. "But I'll finish it if we get into it. I'd much rather live peacefully, but she's a shrew at times. You'd have to be there to understand."

"Let's slow things down," I suggested. "I suspect that beneath your obvious anger there's a whole world of hurt. Based on the way you talk to each other, you both must be struggling. My guess is that you're hurt and confused. It's obvious that you're going to need to learn some skills if you're going to solve these problems and get out of this crisis."

"That's why we're here," Tammie said. "We fight about stupid things—the way we spend money, the way we treat our grandkids, even where we go on vacation. These last few years we've become more and more sarcastic with each other. It's so hurtful."

Dale rolled his eyes and sighed as Tammie was talking.

"Why did you roll your eyes, Dale?" I asked.

"We've talked like this for years. I've put up with her criticism since the beginning and finally decided I couldn't do it anymore. Changing is going to be harder than you think."

After listening to Dale and Tammie, I imagined their home being a war zone. I imagined them breaking every guideline we've discussed in this book about creating safety and security. I imagined them not guarding their tongues and certainly not planting positive seeds that would help build their marriage.

"I can help you," I said, "but you've got to be willing to change. That's going to mean learning skills that may be very foreign to you. We're going to need to address how to talk to one another, how to listen to one another, and how to treat one another. Are you up for that?"

Both seemed to soften.

"That's why we're here," Tammie said again.

We had our work cut out for us. I was able to slow things down and begin teaching them the basic strategies that every couple needs. Fortunately, it became apparent that they wanted to save their marriage. In fact, they surprised me with their willingness to learn new skills. It was hard work, but we made steady progress because they were willing to try.

The Way We Listen

I reviewed several critical concepts with Tammie and Dale. I challenged them to do three things immediately: stop, look, and listen—skills they were taught in grade school but had forgotten along the way.

"Everything builds on these skills," I said. "If you can master them, you're well on your way to ending this crisis and living a wonderful life."

Stop. I encouraged Tammie and Dale to stop what they were doing. Both admitted they could be sarcastic and unkind. They would never be able to solve their problem unless they stopped what they were currently doing. They had to interrupt their pattern of relating so we could introduce new patterns.

Look. Look around. Pay attention. I challenged Tammie and Dale to notice what they were doing and saying, as well as the impact it was having on others. Paying attention is a powerful behavior changer because simply noticing our destructive patterns is the first step in repairing damaged relationships.

When we pay complete attention, absorbing the full effect of our words on our mate, we often feel empathy for them. Sometimes we feel appropriate guilt and inner conviction. We see the pain we're causing by our inattentiveness and rejection.

Listen. Listen to what you're saying and what your mate is saying. What is the feedback you're receiving from your mate, from friends and family, and from God? You're getting information all the time, and it can transform your life if you take the time to examine what you are hearing.

Before listening, someone has to speak. In this book, you've learned how to create a sacred space to share thoughts and feelings. People must feel safe and expect to be attended to if they are going to bare their soul. Given a safe space in which to speak, people are usually willing to share their thoughts, feelings, and desires.

Listening has been considered the highest compliment we can pay someone. Truly attending to what our mate says and expressing a genuine interest in their concerns is a remarkable act of love.

Having listened to our mate, we open ourselves to being influenced by them. What's the point in their sharing their heart with us if we merely offer a quick rebuttal, change the subject, or vehemently disagree?

True listening leads to empathy, and empathy leads to understanding. Only when we understand our mate can we be open to change within us.

Recently, Christie asked for my attention. She was clearly distraught, so I scooted my chair next to hers, asking what she wanted to talk about. Without prejudging her or needing her to take a certain position, I simply listened. I didn't like everything I heard, but I set my feelings aside to create a space for her to share her heart.

"David," she said tearfully. "I'm overwhelmed with all the driving I'm doing because it's leaving too little time for us to be together. This isn't the life I imagined living when we got married. I think I'm going to drop a class or two so we can spend more time together."

A part of me didn't want her to drop a class because I knew it would only mean a delay in the completion of her schooling. But that was what she needed to do, and I set my feelings aside. This wasn't a time for me to try to solve a problem, explore other solutions, or dissuade her from her feelings. She'd have shut down. I didn't interfere, she didn't shut down, and we shared a special moment.

Listening means putting our egos aside. Any need for control, manipulation, or coercion must be harnessed. Attending to our mate must be moved to center stage. This is not easy to do, especially during a crisis.

The Way We Speak

Our language, including the way we speak to our mate, sets the tone and temperature for our home and marriage. If our speech is kind and sensitive, we create a warm and caring environment. If, on the other hand, our speech is harsh and insensitive, marital crisis is far more likely to occur.

The tongue has always been a problem for people, especially couples in crisis. The apostle James had it right when he said, "Likewise the tongue is a small part of the body, but it makes great boasts. Consider what a great forest is set on fire by a small spark. The tongue is also a fire, a world of evil among the parts of the body. It corrupts the whole person, sets the whole course of his life on fire, and is itself on fire by hell" (James 3:5-6).

Who hasn't experienced this "hell" caused by the tongue? We don't want to cause damage, but when we are hurt, frustrated, or irritable, we're tempted to say nearly anything, which often leads to disaster.

In spite of knowing, intellectually at least, that we cannot hurl insults at our mate and expect them to continue loving us, we bubble forth with anger without regard for the consequences. Even knowing that our mate is desperate for love and affection, we're too often gruff and insensitive with our remarks. Though we know that we are called to be people of peace, we too often let trivial matters affect us. Willard Harley, in his book *Love Busters,* declares anger a major culprit in marriage crises.

> This emotion overrides intelligence, which knows that punishment usually doesn't solve problems; it only makes the

> people you punish angry and often causes them to want to inflict punishment on you...When you become angry with your spouse, you have failed to protect your spouse. Anger, which wants to hurt the one you love, wins out over intelligence, which wants to provide your spouse safety and security. When anger wins, romantic love loses.[2]

Although anger is certainly a normal emotion, rarely do we follow the biblical imperative, "In your anger do not sin" (Ephesians 4:26). Listening to our anger without letting it scream in our ears is difficult. We must remember that anger is a secondary emotion—if you're going to manage your anger, you'll need to tune in to the feelings that lie beneath it.

Anger is the aggressive, powerful emotion that covers our underlying wounded feelings. Anger is the muscular bodyguard that shouts, "I'm not going to let you hurt me or make me feel small and insignificant." Anger bursts onto the scene to guard our insecurities and cover our sadness or pain. Once we recognize these vulnerable emotions and attend to them, we won't need anger to serve as our guard.

Anger and the way we speak lead to other problems, such as "thinking errors," which in turn create havoc in a relationship. See if any of these errors, taken from my book *See Dick and Jane Grow Up,* exist in your marriage:

- Universalizing: making an unwarranted leap from a specific situation to a vast generalization by using such words as *always* and *never.*
- Character killing: switching from issues related to the current conflict to personal attacks on your mate.
- Cloud covering: making vague accusations instead of being detailed and specific about a complaint.
- Upping the ante: responding to your spouse by playing tit for tat, citing a worse case that's been done to you.
- Scatter bombing: dropping a huge list of sins into the conversation.

- Mothballing: putting an old grievance in storage for years or decades and bringing it out just at the right time to hurt your mate.
- Spitting in your soup: Using passive-aggressive comments to lay a guilt trip on your mate, often through sarcasm.[3]

Who among us hasn't resorted to these relationship killers? As you navigate through your marriage crisis, you'll undoubtedly see some of these bombs in your relationship. The good news is that if you can identify them, you can change them. Seeing these patterns and taking responsibility for them is the first step.

But exactly how can you change your speech?

- Speak the truth in love. What would happen if you checked everything you said to ensure that your motive for saying it was to love? Imagine how loving speech, even when conveying something that might be critical, might transform your marriage.
- Empathize with your mate. Empathy is the bridge we build to our mate when endeavoring to walk in their shoes. By listening to them and then sharing what we've heard, we forge a strong bond of trust. Sharing empathy encourages our mate to share even more with us, creating a deeper, richer relationship.
- Speak words of encouragement. Our mate needs words of encouragement—especially during a crisis. They need to hear us say things that build them up according to their most pressing needs. They need a cheerleader, not a critic.
- Speak words of humor. A little levity during these tough times will add ballast to our listing boat. Humor provides perspective to an otherwise dark situation. As the old line goes, "The situation is hopeless but not serious." Smile!
- Speak life! There is power in our words. The Scriptures indicate that by our words we will be acquitted or condemned (Matthew 12:37). Through our words, we encourage our mate and our marriage, or we condemn our mate and our

marriage. Choose to speak positive life and encouragement into your marriage.

Although this is only a partial list of ways in which your words can strengthen your marriage, practicing these simple strategies can change the direction of your relationship.

The Way We Behave

Having challenged you in the areas of listening and speaking, let me offer my final instruction: Change the way you behave.

Couples in crisis often focus so much on raising a family, paying bills, and transporting kids to soccer that they forget to have fun. They forget to do the simple things that bring delight to a relationship, such as offering to help one another, buying surprise gifts, and getting away for vacations. They let their church attendance slip and their spiritual life dry up.

Reviving your marriage requires a change of behavior. In fact, if you change the way you behave, your emotions are likely to follow. Your good deed often begets a good deed by your mate. One kindness leads to another. Soon, you've strung together a necklace of kindnesses that can transform a relationship.

Alexandra Stoddard, author of *Gracious Living in a New World,* emphasizes the importance of graceful living. She talks about both her marriage and Stonington Village, where she and her husband reside:

> We know that we need each other to make this little society work. We need each other to survive...We take care of each other when there is an illness or death, and we take pride in one another's achievements as well...We are not only physically interdependent, but spiritually too. When people do good for each other, the whole town feels blessed.[4]

Each of us has the power to create a wonderful, life-giving community in our marriage and family. We do this by the way we listen, talk, and behave. Everything we do matters.

Putting It All Together

Instead of living in crisis mode, fighting bitterly and failing to create a safe place to listen and speak lovingly to one another, Tammie and Dale began practicing the skills discussed in this chapter. They noticed troubling patterns and ended them. They spoke affectionately to each other, listened carefully, and were able to move beyond their crisis.

They also learned a powerful tool—*mutuality.* Simply put, you tend to get back what you give to others. When Tammie spoke bitterly to Dale, he often spoke bitterly in return. If she wanted love and affection, she needed to offer those same qualities to him. You cannot continue to attack your mate and then expect him or her to treat you kindly.

We attack enemies, not those we love. We create safety with our mate so we can share vulnerable feelings, even if only to say, "I need more love and support from you."

Tammie and Dale gradually learned to listen to the feelings below the feelings. Instead of lashing out in anger, for example, they shared the pain they felt and asked the other to attend and listen to those feelings. They gradually built a safe place where they could share their wounds and attend to them lovingly. Listening attentively, speaking kind and truthful words, and behaving in a gentle manner transformed their marriage.

Tammie and Dale also decided to begin attending their old church again. Here, in the safety of the sanctuary, they once again held hands, sang familiar hymns, and listened to the preaching of God's Word. God began His work in their hearts, encouraging them to love one another in spite of the wounds they'd suffered. Today, they are on their way to creating a healthy and loving relationship. I am confident they will emerge from their marriage crisis stronger than ever.

10

Staying on the Road to Recovery

"For I know the plans I have for you," declares the LORD, "plans to prosper you and not to harm you, plans to give you a hope and a future."

JEREMIAH 29:11

The sirens are silent, the crisis has passed. From the ambulance crew to the emergency room staff, everyone had a single focus: to stabilize the patient and aid in her recovery.

The woman with the fractured hip is doing well. She was taken to surgery, where an orthopedic surgeon performed an operation he's done hundreds of times before, pinning her leg in several places, preparing her for convalescence, and placing orders for her long-term care and rehabilitation. She's gone from immediate crisis to stabilization and is on the road to recovery.

A marital crisis is much the same as a medical crisis: We must work quickly and sometimes urgently to stabilize a relationship, creating trust before we can begin long-term recovery. In a crisis, our focus is on the here and now—stabilize, create security, and allow no further damage.

Marital crises rarely erupt out of thin air. In fact, as we've seen, if they are predictable, as many crises are, they are also preventable, and that is the focus of our final chapter. But first, let's review the ten lifesavers that will help you on your road to recovery:

- Emergencies force us to pay attention, placing us on red alert with all systems heightened to prepare for the medical or marital emergency.
- Emergencies require that we narrow our focus, causing no further damage as we seek stability before making any long-range plans.
- Emergencies require that we create safety and that we understand that violations to that safety inhibit and jeopardize the healing process.
- Emergencies require that we establish trust. This fragile bond of trust can be damaged easily and can require much work to restore.
- Emergencies demand that we learn about what led up to the emergency before we can begin to deal effectively with our issues.
- Emergencies are wake-up calls that offer us opportunities to adjust our lives to address problems within our marriage and to determine what is most important to us.
- Emergencies, once stabilized, require that we eliminate barriers to change and manage situations that could lead to even more crises in the future.
- Emergencies alert us to what is already strong within our marriage and give us opportunities to build upon those strengths.
- Emergencies require that we learn skills we are missing so a marital emergency doesn't recur.
- Emergencies, after the initial crisis, require that we begin rehabilitation with a focus on long-term recovery.

Initially assisted by the ambulance crew and then by the emergency room staff, the woman with the fractured hip is now settled into a life of recovery. She attends physical therapy and is strengthening her leg and hip. Challenged daily not to start believing that her work is finished, she is told by doctors and therapists that if she will continue to push herself, she'll regain normal, healthy functioning.

Although the immediate crisis may be over, her future depends on the decisions she makes today. She can attempt to shorten her immediate crisis by taking shortcuts and avoiding physical therapy, or she can determine to make wiser choices that will propel her toward a full and healthy life in the future.

Like the woman with the fractured hip, you too face decisions that will impact your future. Will you work diligently to stabilize your marriage? Will you earnestly seek to create and maintain safety? Most importantly, will you move beyond the immediate crisis and seek to eliminate barriers to change, thus creating a healthier marriage in the future?

A life-changing course of action is available to you. It includes managing your emotions, learning about the factors that led to this particular crisis, and eradicating problematic relational patterns.

Keeping the End in Sight

The road to recovery involves immediate decisions to stabilize, secure, and establish trust. It also includes making plans for your future. Ending one crisis offers no assurance of future safety unless strategic steps are taken, and we want to make those clear in this last chapter.

With one eye on the immediate problems and another on making provisions for the future, we move forward. With part of our energy on practicing the new skills in the here and now and another part on considering preventive strategies, we navigate our personal road to recovery.

Stephen Covey, in his book *The Seven Habits of Highly Effective People,* teaches that effective people always keep their desired goals in sight, even when dealing with immediate problems. By focusing on the end, they can choose those activities that will help them accomplish their desired goals.

An experience I had several years ago illustrates how *not* to do things. On a crisp, fall Saturday morning, runners began gathering in Longview, Washington. The mood was cheerful and light, with friends offering encouragement. I had signed up for my first Harvest Fun Run, an event to kick off the fall season. Many of those present told me they had been doing these runs for years. This was my first.

I hadn't prepared for the 10K race. And yet, in spite of my lack of training, I actually believed I had a chance to win my age division! I was fit, I reasoned, and 10K was only six miles. I enjoyed running and had always been an above-average athlete. So along with celebrating the harvest season, I planned to pull off an upset of the more established runners. How tough could it be?

I was incredibly naive, arrogant, and foolish to consider this a possibility—but that's precisely what I was thinking.

Pulsing with adrenaline, I shot out from the starting line and began sprinting ahead of most of the other runners. By the half-mile mark, only the veteran runners were hanging with me. Still running well at the one- and two-mile marks, I had plenty of energy and was more confident than ever that I could win my age division.

As I neared the three-mile mark, however, I began to feel winded. With increasing difficulty I pushed myself until my breathing became more and more labored and I began to feel sick to my stomach. My lungs ached, my chest heaved, my stomach churned, and I started to get light-headed. I had hit the wall.

Having once overheard someone talking about the need to "run through the pain," I did my best to ignore the signals my body was sending. A few more yards, however, and there was no question that I had to stop. I was done. Out of breath, sick to my stomach, and humiliated, I stepped out of the way of the other runners and leaned against a tree, holding my stomach.

After several minutes, I began to feel slightly better and was able to walk slowly to the finish line. So much for winning my age group. I came in dead last—and I felt dead. I had made a colossal error:

failure to keep the end in mind. I underestimated the challenges and overestimated my ability to handle them. I suffered for it.

Twin Pillars of Failure

I made many errors during that 10K debacle, all of them the result of failing to consider the big picture. This is an error common not only to neophyte athletes but also to those in the midst of a marriage crisis. Let's explore these errors a bit more closely.

Arrogance

I was incredibly arrogant to assume that I had a shot at winning my division in my first 10K. How could I have possibly believed I could defeat seasoned, trained athletes? In retrospect, it was preposterous for me to think I could compete against runners who understood the challenges of competitive racing. I hadn't taken the time to learn anything about racing or to do any training. My expectations were completely unrealistic.

Picking up the broken pieces of my pride, I recalled the apostle Paul's admonition: "Everyone who competes in the games goes into strict training...do not run like a man running aimlessly" (1 Corinthians 9:25-26). I'm sure that if he'd observed my approach to the race, Paul would have been concerned about me.

His philosophy applies directly to managing marriage crises. We must take the time to learn everything possible about the problems, about our role in them, and about what it takes to come out the other side better than ever.

I'm amazed by the number of couples who believe they can simply learn a few new tricks and then expect to overcome their crisis. Years of troubling behavior brought them to this point, and their patterns are firmly entrenched. But in their minds, a little healing tonic and a few prayers should be enough to fix any problem.

It just isn't so. Successfully coping with and overcoming a marital crisis with only a few pain-free steps is as unlikely as winning a 10K simply by wishing and hoping you can.

This kind of self-confidence is foolish. Your best thinking and planning got you into this mess, and it will take a whole lot more than self-confidence to get you out of it.

I walked the last few miles of the race, clutching my side and stomach, hoping no one had noticed my embarrassing antics during the first leg of the run. I was experiencing a huge dose of humility—a great antidote to arrogance.

The apostle James reminds us, "God opposes the proud, but gives grace to the humble" (James 4:6). How true it is! I felt humbled and humiliated, but humility was a great teacher. I learned an enduring lesson that day.

Jesus, of course, is our greatest teacher of appropriate humility. The Scriptures tell us that we are to have the same attitude as Christ Jesus, "who, being in very nature God, did not consider equality with God something to be grasped, but made himself nothing, taking the very nature of a servant, being made in human likeness" (Philippians 2:6-7).

During a crisis, it is important that you not wrap yourself in false pride, believing that you can conquer the problem on your own. You'll need expert counsel, support, and specific plans for change.

Fear

The second pillar of failure is our fear of being unable to make changes. As I explored my failure in the Harvest Run, I discovered some problems that went beyond my ability to complete a 10K race. I had bypassed the hard work and foolishly jumped into competitive racing without doing the necessary preparation. Afraid of landing in the back of the pack, I lunged to the head of the race—at least for a few miles.

Black-and-white thinking either causes us to believe we can't make progress or leads us to believe we can do anything. There is error in both positions. Afraid that nothing will ever change, we often deny our problems or simply give up because we feel overwhelmed. If we opt for overconfidence, we rush ahead without adequate regard for the severity of the situation.

I spoke recently with a woman who is considering marriage. Shelly is a sharp-dressing 50-year-old with red hair. Previously divorced, she has been dating Hal for some time. Shelly shared the following problems during her first appointment.

"My emotions are all over the map. Most of the time I think Hal is a great guy, and I'm ready to marry him. He can convince me that we have a wonderful relationship, and to a certain extent it's true. But he's got some problems that never go away. Every time I think they're gone, they resurface."

"Please explain," I said.

"To begin with, he's not honest with me," she said. "He tells me he'll be over at eight in the evening and then shows up at nine with a bunch of excuses. If it happened once in a while, that might be okay, but that's not the case."

"In what other ways is he dishonest with you?"

"He told me he'd be willing to sit down with me to talk about our future, but when I bring up the fact that we've been dating a year and still haven't discussed our life together, he says he doesn't remember making that agreement. There are plenty of other examples of the same type of behavior. It drives me crazy."

"Do you hold him accountable for these agreements?"

"When I confront him, he gets angry. I'm afraid to push too hard because I know he'll get irritated."

"So you just give in and go along with things?"

"I suppose that's true," she said. "I'm always annoyed with Hal and with myself. We haven't talked for the past three days, and our relationship is ready to fall apart. I love him, but I'm afraid of confronting our problems. When I try, he tells me I'm too demanding and threatens to end the relationship."

Shelly vacillated between naïveté—believing that everything was going to be fine—and fear—believing that nothing could be changed.

This black-and-white thinking left her stuck. Her solution was to face the fact that she and Hal needed to do significant work.

Sustaining Momentum

Fear and arrogance are guaranteed to create roadblocks on your road to recovery. Fear will stop you dead in your tracks, and arrogance will propel you headlong in the wrong direction.

Keeping a balanced perspective is the primary survival skill in maintaining momentum on the road to recovery. Life is not hopeless, nor is the sky the limit. Your marriage is not doomed, nor should you expect to skate easily through the months ahead. Momentum is fueled by realistic hope and a clear, decisive plan.

A balanced perspective includes managing your immediate crisis and employing the skills covered in this book while preparing for the months and years ahead. It means not allowing yourself to naively expect a bright future. It also means not allowing yourself to slip into discouragement. This balance is hard to find and even harder to maintain.

An integral aspect of maintaining a balanced perspective involves *pace.* Pacing yourself means being watchful. You find your own rhythm by focusing on today while keeping an eye on tomorrow. There will be days when you must deal with immediate issues, and other days when you can sit back and enjoy the gains you've made.

You wouldn't be reading this book if you weren't interested in saving your marriage, so let's build on that commitment. Nothing of substance, and this certainly includes marriage, is created and sustained without perseverance and momentum. Although we live in a society that expects instant results and gratification, this attitude simply does not work when we apply it to marriage.

Consider these practical steps for sustaining momentum toward your goal:

- Clarify your commitment. You're married but experiencing a crisis. Still, you want to work it out. Make this clear to one another. Remind your mate that you still want to be married and want to develop the long-term skills needed to live happily ever after.

- Acknowledge that the road to recovery will not be smooth. Progress never has been linear, and it never will be. There are fits and starts, potholes and hurdles, tragedies and triumphs. Verbalize this process to one another. A setback doesn't equal failure.
- Regroup after setbacks. Review your recipe for success, reminding yourself of the tools and strategies you need to master.
- Acknowledge gains. Take time to pat yourselves on the back and note the skills you've learned. This is a time to celebrate and build on the strengths you've developed over the life of your marriage.
- Take a realistic appraisal of where you are today, tallying gains and losses, mistakes and smart choices, failures and successes. Realistically determine what areas still need work, with an eye on avoiding future crises and moving forward in your relationship.

Momentum is sustained by planting seeds and then trusting they will germinate and grow. You've decided to make your marriage work, and these seeds of faith will be fruitful. You're committed to practicing the skills discussed in this book, and gradually they will revolutionize your marriage.

Working the Plan and Planning the Work

Naively hoping for change, without a clear strategy, doesn't work. Each tool, every technique, all the suggestions offered thus far in this book comprise your game plan, the strategy designed to end your crisis and move you forward into a healthy, stable, and loving marriage. Nothing is mysterious about this—it works.

You can do many things to improve your marriage, but let's review what we've covered in this book so you can construct a plan to suit your particular situation. Your plan must be specific, agreed upon by both, with some sort of accountability. Working with a trained professional is likely to help you maintain focus. If you follow the guidelines in this book, you create every possibility for success. If you approach this task haphazardly, shifting into either an arrogant position or cowering beneath an attitude of paralyzed fearfulness, you will surely fail.

There is an incredible tendency to drift through life like a leaf on a river, going wherever the current takes us. If, however, you make firm plans and work your plan, you'll be prepared for many possibilities. Rather than being like a leaf at the whim of the currents, you can equip yourself with both paddle and canoe. You can choose where you want your life and your marriage to go.

In many ways, to drift is easier than to take responsibility for working a plan. After all, if things don't go well and you find yourself in another crisis, you can blame your spouse, God, or fate. But if you really want things to go well, and most of us do, you must develop a plan and work it. You must set a direction for your marriage, discuss it with your spouse, and stick to it.

Dr. John Gottman, author of *The Seven Principles for Making Your Marriage Work,* discusses the importance of knowing your mate intimately, which helps when mapping out your plan. "Emotionally intelligent couples are intimately familiar with each other's world." This includes knowing the issues likely to cause problems in the marriage and constructing a plan to deal with them.[1]

This morning, Christie and I had just such a conversation. With my feet up on my desk, relaxed and peaceful, and her sitting cross-legged with a hot cup of tea, we discussed where our relationship is going and where we want to be a year from now. Like sailors plotting a course, we mulled the possibilities aloud.

Having come through a challenging time in our marriage when we were both cross with one another (primarily because we were going too many directions and being too busy), we both wanted to make plans for slowing down. I said that I was ready to downsize, possibly selling our larger home, on the condition that we create a special place for my grand piano. Christie was at first cool to that idea, but she warmed up as we discussed the possibilities. She said that she wanted less stress, and putting off remodeling our cabin would help her with that.

We have a plan and intend to work it. We don't want to drift, and we certainly don't want any crises in our marriage. We're not naive, however. We know that trouble comes quickly when we don't attend to our plans. Drifting back into busyness, materialism, and preoccupation is all too easy. We don't want those things to crowd out our special time for one another. They can—but only if we let them.

Anticipating and Averting Crises

"To fail to plan is to plan to fail." This popular saying is so true. There's a crisis around the corner for each of us if we don't ferociously guard our lives. I don't want to create panic or paranoia, but you should know that just because you've navigated your way out of one crisis does not mean another isn't waiting in the wings.

I'm simply reminding you of a stark reality—bad things happen to those who don't learn from their mistakes. Your challenge now is to take inventory, know where your potholes lie, and then avoid them.

The great news is that most marital crises can be avoided with appropriate planning and follow-through. Do you know the weak spots in your marriage? Are you working to strengthen them? Do you have someone you check in with, such as a pastor or counselor, who will help keep you on track? These are a few of the ways you can avert disaster.

Perhaps the greatest advice I can give on averting crises in your marriage is simply this: Keep the slate clean. Unresolved anger, hurt, bitterness, and resentment create an atmosphere that will put you on the brink of a marital meltdown. An accumulation of bad feelings can surface at the most inopportune time. Left unresolved, bad feelings eventually lead to an explosion, and a few explosions can lead to a full-blown crisis.

Dedication to Continual Growth

You will never arrive. I hate to disappoint you, but you'll never get to a place in your marriage where you can coast. You'll never get to a point where you're done growing. Thankfully, you'll also never get to a place where your marriage is done growing. It can always get better.

One of my greatest hopes for couples facing marriage crises is that they grasp the hope and belief that their relationship can be so much more than it is today. However, to maintain this growth requires an uncommon dedication. It is easy to get side-tracked or to naively believe that growth will happen without work.

As a psychologist working with an in-patient drug and alcohol program, I watched dozens of well-intentioned men and women leave the unit, vowing to stay clean and sober, only to end up back with us months later. In fact, so common were the relapses that we began seeing our treatment program as a revolving door.

Although there are many, many reasons for relapse, one of the most common is not being dedicated to growth. "If you're not in recovery," we'd say, "you're in relapse." Stated another way, if you're not dedicated to moving forward, you're losing ground.

Scott Peck shouts out this truth, declaring that love is largely a matter of self-discipline. While the gushy aspects of love are made of biochemical and emotional elements, he asserts that real, lasting love involves being dedicated to the well-being of yourself and your mate. "Any genuine lover behaves with self-discipline and any genuinely loving relationship is a disciplined relationship."[2] Healthy love doesn't just happen on its own.

Love involves dedicating yourself to others' well-being and to your own. We dare not get swept away in the fuzzy sentimentalism of romance as portrayed on television. There will be downfalls and disappointments, and our mate, like us, may never be all that we'd hoped they'd be—but they can be more than enough. We can find the balance of what we need in our relationship with ourselves and God.

The road to marital recovery is established when we are dedicated to growing spiritually, emotionally, and relationally. If you will dedicate yourself to attending to your mate's likes, dislikes, weaknesses, and strengths, as well as your own, and if you are committed to enriching them, you'll save yourself a lot of heartache and enjoy a wonderful marriage.

Staying the Course

You have good reason to be confident. You're learning how to stabilize your marriage crisis, you understand the importance of safety, and you are rebuilding trust with your mate. You recognize the strengths that still exist in your marriage and realize the importance of building on them. You're also working to establish and implement a plan that incorporates many of the skills discussed in this book. With those skills firmly in place, you have every reason to stay the course.

The apostle Paul tells us, "Let us not become weary in doing good, for at the proper time we will reap a harvest if we do not give up" (Galatians 6:9).

As you navigate your marital crisis and attempt to sail toward a more rewarding future, you must find a way to keep an even keel. You'll make yourself sick if you make too much of the daily vacillations that occur in your marriage. No couple can maintain a blissful relationship every day, nor can they remain unaffected when things go sideways.

We're only human, but we can continue to do the good things we've learned to do. You have a powerful recipe to fall back on, and if you continue to use it, you're going to be fine. As you stay the course, remember these two final thoughts:

1. Remember that the path of love is not for the squeamish. There are no perfect marriages—none. Your pastor, believe it or not, has had his or her own struggles. I know this to be true, and you'd do well to remind yourself of it. We're all just doing the best we can, and if you

can stand back and realize that your situation is more the norm than the exception, you'll fare much better.

2. Every problem has its silver lining. This sounds like a grandmother's advice, but it's true. You can find a lesson in every struggle. As the apostle James says, "Consider it pure joy, my brothers, whenever you face trials of many kinds" (James 1:3). If you are receptive to learning, you can stand back and smile when a new struggle comes your way.

When all else fails, stay the course. When you're uncertain about how to react to the latest challenge in your marriage, stay the course. When you're tempted to give up and abandon the road to recovery, stay the course.

If you stay the course and do your best, your marriage can prosper.

Notes

Chapter 1—Recognizing a State of Emergency

1. John Gottman, *Why Marriages Succeed or Fail* (New York: Simon & Schuster, 1994), 75.
2. Robert Fulgham, *All I Really Need to Know I Learned in Kindergarten* (New York: Villard Books, 1988), 6.

Chapter 3—Creating Safety

1. Willard F. Harley Jr., *His Needs, Her Needs* (Grand Rapids: Fleming Revell, 1986), 16.

Chapter 4—Establishing Trust

1. Cherie Carter-Scott, *If Love Is a Game, These Are the Rules* (New York: Broadway Books, 1999), 21.
2. William J. Bennett, *The Book of Virtues* (New York: Simon & Schuster, 1998), 665.
3. Dr. David Schnarch, *Passionate Marriage* (New York: Henry Holt, 1997), 404.

Chapter 5—Determining the Causes of Your Crisis

1. Adapted from *The Medical Journal of Australia.* www.mja.com.au/public/mental health/articles/rosen/rosen.html.
2. Stephanie Dowrick, *Forgiveness and Other Acts of Love* (New York: Norton, 1997), 71.

Chapter 6—Responding to Your Wake-Up Call

1. M. Scott Peck, *The Road Less Traveled* (New York: Simon & Schuster, 1978), 44.
2. Michele Weiner Davis, *The Divorce Remedy* (New York: Simon & Schuster, 2001), 62.
3. Robert S. Pasick, *Awakening from the Deep Sleep* (New York: HarperSanFrancisco, 1992), 107-11.

Chapter 7—Eliminating Barriers to Change

1. Chuck Swindoll, *Dropping Your Guard* (Dallas: Word, 1983), 28.
2. Patricia Love, *The Truth About Love* (New York: Simon & Schuster, 2001), 60.
3. Chris Thurman, "The Truth About Change," *Today's Better Life,* Summer 1992, 41.

Chapter 8—Strengthening the Positive

1. Harville Hendrix, *Getting the Love You Want* (New York: Henry Holt, 1988), 88-89.
2. Hendrix, *Getting the Love You Want,* 208.
3. David E. Clarke, *A Marriage After God's Own Heart* (Sisters, OR: Multnomah, 2001), 115.

Chapter 9—Mastering the Skills

1. Ben Zander and Rosamund Zander, *The Art of Possibility* (New York: Penguin Books, 2000), 111.

2. Willard Harley, *Love Busters* (Grand Rapids: Baker, 1992), 28.

3. David Hawkins, *See Dick and Jane Grow Up* (Colorado Springs: Cook Communications, 2001), 52.

4. Alexandra Stoddard, *Gracious Living in a New World* (New York: William Morrow, 1996), 24.

Chapter 10—Staying on the Road to Recovery

1. John Gottman, *The Seven Principles for Making Your Marriage Work* (New York: Three Rivers Press, 1999), 48.

2. M. Scott Peck, *The Road Less Traveled* (New York: Simon & Schuster, 1978), 155.

Other Great Harvest House Books by Dr. David Hawkins

(To read sample chapters, visit www.harvesthousepublishers.com.)

When Pleasing Others Is Hurting You

When you begin to forfeit your own God-given calling and identity in an unhealthy desire to please others, you move from servanthood to codependency. This helpful guide can get you back on track.

Dealing with the CrazyMakers in Your Life

People who live in chaos and shrug off responsibility can drive you crazy. If you are caught up in a disordered person's life, Dr. Hawkins helps you set boundaries, confront the behavior, and find peace.

Nine Critical Mistakes Most Couples Make

Dr. Hawkins shows that complex relational problems usually spring from nine destructive habits couples fall into, and he offers practical suggestions for changing the way husbands and wives relate to each other.

When Trying to Change Him Is Hurting You

Dr. Hawkins offers practical suggestions for women who want to improve the quality of their relationships by helping the men in their lives become healthier and more fun to live with.

When the Man in Your Life Can't Commit

With empathy and insight Dr. Hawkins uncovers the telltale signs of commitment failure, why the problem exists, and how you can respond to create a life with the commitment-phobic man you love.

Are You Really Ready for Love

As a single, you are faced with a challenge: When love comes your way, will you be ready? Dr. Hawkins encourages you to spend less energy looking for the perfect mate and more energy becoming a person who can enter wholeheartedly into intimate relationships.

The Relationship Doctor's Prescription for Living Beyond Guilt
Dr. Hawkins explains the difference between real guilt, false guilt, shame, and conviction, bringing these feelings into the light and demonstrating how they can reveal the true causes of emotional pain.

The Relationship Doctor's Prescription for Better Communication in Your Marriage
Communication is an art. Couples thrive when they listen deeply, understand completely, and validate one another compassionately. But many couples try to win arguments, not to understand each other. This user-friendly manual reveals common but ineffective patterns of relating and teaches new skills in the art of communication.

The Relationship Doctor's Prescription for Building Your Child's Self-Image
Dr. Hawkins describes what positive self-image is, what it is not, and how to help kids develop a Christlike confidence without conceit. You'll find practical descriptions of children's psychological needs, harmful parenting habits to avoid, and constructive ways to help your children build a healthy self-image.

How to Get Your Husband's Attention
She says one thing, but he hears something entirely different. What can you do to bridge the communication gap? This inspiring guide provides straightforward answers and practical solutions to encourage and motivate you to press through to the ultimate goal: greater intimacy in marriage. (Rerelease of *Saying It So He'll Listen*)

The Power of Emotional Decision Making
"Energy in motion"—that's how Dr. Hawkins describes emotions. He shows how emotions can help you discern what is most important, determine what is missing in your life, and discover how God is leading you in new directions.

Breaking Everyday Addictions
Addiction is a rapidly growing problem among Christians and non-Christians alike. Even socially acceptable behaviors, such as shopping, eating, working, playing, and exercising can quietly take over and ruin lives. This enlightening exposé provides the tools you need to allow the healing power of Christ to permeate your life.